TABLE OF CONTENT

Security Industry Review

The Security Industry Authority (SIA) is the governing body responsible for regulating the private security industry in the UK. It is a non-departmental public body reporting to the Home Secretary, established in 2003 under the terms of the Private Security Act 2001.

The two main responsibilities of this organisation is the licensing of individual sector workers and the management of the voluntary Approved Contractor Scheme (ACS) which measures security suppliers against an independently assessed criteria.

The SIA, by the introduction of regulation, has implemented an ethos of raising standards. They have to some extent achieved this, mostly due to the lack of regulation before licensing was introduced. However due to what I believe may have been the hasty implementation of licensing criteria in order to rapidly issue licenses, some of the training may fall short.

It should be understood by all in the industry, by both employers and the individual license holders, that the licensing criteria and issue of such is that of entry level and further training and experience should be obtained. Unfortunately this is often not the case, employers sometimes avoid offering training in order to reduce costs, and as wage compression hits this industry and the individual hard, we need to move away from this outlook and take stock of our roles and operational requirements. Not just seek out training for the sake of it but actually understand what our jobs entail, the risks involved to ourselves, our clients and the public in general.

The SIA and Home Office would increase the standard if some of the revenue from licensing was made available to subsidise additional training, or at least recognise those that obtain a higher individual standard by a reduction in license fee.

Regardless of this, and not wishing to incentivize training, the raising of standards should be something we all seek to implement. Taking the basics of the foundation and building on it not only increases industry professionalism and the pride of self improvement but it also promotes the principle of minimizing risk, whilst increasing the value of the officer. We are at the end of the day a protective service.

Company Policy

All companies have guidance and operational policies by which they implement their services. These policies may take the form of a mission statement laying out the companies objectives, codes of practice or conduct and even points which may be referred to as standing orders or standard operating procedures. If the company premises is open to the public, or allows access during specific periods, it should also have a company policy with regard to admission. Company policies and the knowledge of such by the workforce allows all staff to understand the vision of the business and focus on that success.

However in regard to policies which are policed by SIA licensed security personnel, such as those relating to admission or conduct, it is of paramount importance that the staff enforcing these policies not only know and understand them but that they also comply legally taking into account the use of the land or premises. Many premises which offer services and are open to the public do often use generic information with regard to admission to the site. Some of which may either not be relevant or in some cases due to the nature of the venue could be unlawful in regard to implementation, especially in locations where access to the site is not controlled and members of the public are initially allowed to roam free. Failing to understand the policies laid out by the company reduces the effectiveness and value of the staff.

As a security professional you are employed by your employer or client to conform to and implement as well as promote adherence to policies laid out by your employer. It is your duty to enforce these terms providing they themselves are lawful. It is your responsibility to know these policies and know if they are lawful in their requests. This is one major difference between those working in a public sector law enforcement role and those who are employed privately to enforce a policy. However by knowing a set of core skills and responsibilities you can confidently assess and flag any issues within the policy document which could be deemed unlawful or be misinterpreted.

If your premises are open to the public one of your primary duties is to inform visitors when they arrive on site. This could be done by placing the policy document in visible locations by the entrance or as a handout to visitors. If this is not practical always be knowledgeable and ready to advise those who breach policy.

As I have said it is your job to understand the policies which you enforce, to know if they are lawful and in the best interests of the company and its vision.

Introduction

The 21st Century has seen many advancements in the security industry. From the introduction of a qualification framework and individual licensing, to the increased workload and expectation placed on those within the industry. With added expectation comes increased responsibility for self reliance and competence falling on all those who hold a SIA license. The industry requires an adaptable workforce, one which understands the need for continual improvement and continuity of service. This can only be achieved from the ground up. The present top down approach has created a starting point for a basic standard of service but without the recognition of the need for continual improvement by those on the front line, it has resulted in the system of continually raising standards stalling and coming to a halt. The need for the industry to come together and implement a little more joined up thinking is long overdue. The time for blaming the legislative process and the government quango put in place to oversee the industry has to end. If an industry is built without first creating an academic framework for the operator, then any educational introduction of such would be considered an improvement to the system. If the industry wishes to build on this it must be the individual license holders and business which take and run with the baton. Accepting an entry level framework without comprehending the need to build on it attracts those people to the industry, both as front line operators and those who start companies, as poorly suited to providing professional good practice. To bring in the best we must understand where improvements need to be made, address them and demonstrate them to others.

The number of operators in the industry continues to increase whereas standards do not, and where on paper two officers may hold the same license their skill and commitment may be poles apart. This book intends to address this, by promoting higher standards and recognising the quality and professionalism of those that understand the gravity of what they are being asked to provide and allowing it to be projected to the wider society.

Having worked in the industry for over 20 years, both full and part time in many different environments, I am well equipped and experienced at assessing situations and understanding both operational and client needs in order to promote safe practice. After a period in the military I felt the logical progressive step was to obtain a Close Protection license but found myself gravitating due to market forces and natural flare towards roles which were primarily assessment focussed or customer orientated and public facing, whilst increasing my subject knowledge and academic skill by undertaking Risk

Management training, along with studies in Criminology, Criminal Justice, Psychology and Law. There are far more with greater experience regarding the aforementioned profession, and it has been extensively written about in recent years. My aptitude for dealing with incidents and all manner of emergencies has seen steady growth of my business and it is from my experience and the things I have witnessed whilst operating that leads me to write this book.

I have throughout my time observed both good practice and bad. There are many professionals in this industry, but on the whole there is a desperate need for improvement across the board. There are places where an understanding of the risks involved is missing, and complacency and resentment for the task runs rampant.

Due to the implementation of licensing it is no longer feasible to only possess a narrow view of the industry. A single set of skills is not a practical approach in a multiple risk environment. The unique dangers faced by security personnel often means that the quality and the calibre of the individual is regularly tested. For that reason it is imperative that the right training and experience is undertaken by all. It is not just about career advancement. It is an issue of personal advancement and safety. A professional will take ownership of this need and facilitate its solution.

With the constant increase in threat towards business and society, more and more is being asked of the security industry. Creating pressure on those in the sector to provide an adaptable highly skilled workforce, capable of operating in any environment, whilst still providing excellence. The aim of this book is to explain some of the basic requirements needed to operate as a public facing security patrol officer in order to minimise risk and promote safety. It will also provide general knowledge of the sector in order to assist those considering entering into this varied industry, and to act as an aide memoir for both new entrants and seasoned professionals, prompting discussion and debate. The material in this book has been laid out in an easily absorbed format and will highlight the need and importance of assessment and situation awareness giving you an understanding of the value of the role, and the needs and requirements of those undertaking this duty.

Due to the varied nature and often ignored complexity of the many roles within the industry it must be pointed out that this book concentrates on basic core skills, ones which should be held by all, regardless of the environment you operate in. It is hoped that the reader will take the information offered and adapt it to the situation and operational requirements of their particular profession.

Contrary to perception it takes a particular person to work in the security industry, many try and fail. Many coast by without being tested but the professional knows the risks and reasons for their importance. Being entrusted with the safety of others is a rewarding and responsible task. If you are given that trust then failing to offer excellence not only increases risk to others but also to yourself. A security professional is just that, a professional, one that is adaptable, forward thinking and able to work under pressure.

A person that takes pride in what they do, how they act and how they respond. One who rises to a challenge, sees problems and formulates solutions while others are still contemplating. A professional is someone who projects confidence in their abilities, reassuring those who look to them.

Understanding the law and taking responsibility for ones own actions cannot be offset to others. Having the confidence to not only know when and how to take action but to act confidently and responsibly and in the best interests of others is what makes for an excellent security officer. The law is the most important weapon of governance for any industry, as you read through this book it will become self evident that a good understanding of this subject will be the main weapon within your arsenal.

Having the ability to quickly assess situations and react in a positive manner, either by taking the lead or working as part of a well trained team is what separates the mediocre from the outstanding. It is not all about natural ability, but rather learning and absorbing knowledge. It is about gaining experience and listening to the right people in order to expand your skill. All things must be learnt, all skill must be honed. Those who are made of the right stuff know that everyday presents new training experiences and new challenges, that is the nature of the industry. It can be varied, but it can also seem at times mundane if opportunities are overlooked. A security professional will make the most of any down time, as they realise that security is not just a means to take your life from point A to point B. For those that operate pay cheque to pay cheque with little concern for the task at hand and who moan about how they are overlooked when it comes to promotion or privilege. They should concern themselves more with the reason why they are overlooked. It may have something to do with the lack of effort or commitment to duty. The professional knows their value, not just in monetary terms but in responsibility. When you are responsible for the safety of others, they rely on you, as do your colleagues. If you fail to give 100% to the task and fail to understand the value of your role and make an effort to improve your skills you are ultimately failing yourself.

Due to constraints this book does not include material in relation to First Aid training. This is not to say that this training has no value. On the contrary, as the book will explain, first aid provision is one of the most important aspects. The reason for its omission from this book is because the subject could not be covered to the extent to which it would need to be. It is advisable if you are lacking this experience or training that you undertake some form of first aid course as soon as possible as this is something that will benefit you and those around you both at work as well as within society.

This book has been written in order to lay out the experiences and views of the author throughout his career within the security industry. It concentrates on the roles and responsibilities of those working in general security and customer service environments. Information held within comes from operational experience and training and from material which is on public record. It discusses the theory and academic merit but also how this relates to practical application. The security industry is diverse in relation to responsibility, but it is also diverse when it comes to response. The attitude and personal approach of the individual officer combined with the training and experience they have received creates a broad spectrum approach to professionalism and quality of service. By understanding the value and importance of the industry, and combining it with a positive philosophy, training material and operational case studies in this book, the reader will understand the legal and operational importance of unifying the approach of those on the front-line.

Whether you work in a public facing role or protect property out of hours this book will cover the core skills needed to deal competently with minimising risk and dealing with incidents. It will give you the confidence to maintain a professional approach by instilling a methodical attitude to operational implementation.

It is is by no means a bible or an oracle containing every detail of information regarding every incident or situation you may come across. It covers fundamental principles and experiences and has been designed to give a benchmark understanding of the skills needed to be a success, removing the blinkered tunnel vision view that many have towards dealing with incidents and task approach. You will learn the importance of assessment and how it relates to your safety and the safety of others, allowing you to rapidly evaluate and respond to dilemmas in a positive manner, building a foundation which will guide your actions and propel you towards creating success. From this book you will take away not only an understanding of the theory combined with the practical; you will also realise your potential, the importance of what you are doing, and the pride and value you bring.

CHAPTER ONE

Core Values

What is security?

Security is defined as; "The degree of resistance to, or protection from harm. It applies to any vulnerable or valuable asset such as a person or property".

Oxford Dictionary

The purpose of the security professional regardless of their individual discipline is to apply counter-measures in order to mitigate against threat and minimise risk. We accomplish this by training, planning and implementing both physical and electronic surveillance measures in order to detect and deter crime and disorder.

A Security officer by their presence is a prominent deterrent providing they know their trade craft.

What makes a good security officer

It may be seen by some that it is an ideal role for those with former military experience or for those that have retired from the police and many from these backgrounds do move into private security, whether that be in a specialist service role or a uniformed guarding/customer facing one.

These professions do offer a certain level of experience that can be easily absorbed and utilised by the industry. However the training and experience of the individual becomes irrelevant if they fail to retain the knowledge they have learnt. I have met many in this industry and like all others there are some which are extremely good and proactive, and there are some that act as jacket fillers and time wasters merely showing up to clock in and clock out and avoid doing any actual work in between.

This occurs in many organisations and it would be naive to think that this can be completely avoided. However if you are one of these types, or work in an environment such as this, it is not just a productivity issue or the financial loss of man hours to be concerned about. It is the very nature of the safety and future of the business you are employed to protect which is at risk.

This includes not just the product or infrastructure but the personnel within the organisation. It should also be remembered that this attitude spreads and creates a culture of "why bother" you see others not doing their jobs so why should I. Well the answer to that is simple and a very selfish one at that. Take a look at your role, the reason we have security officers. We are employed to minimise risk, so consider the risks. Do you deal with volatile situations, aggressive individuals, crime and disorder? Whether these are actual occurrences or just perceived possibilities you have to be able to be relied on and you must be able to rely on those around you to assist or you increase the risk of physical injury. Even your basic license training emphasises the need for support structures. So be all you can not just for others but for yourself.

I have worked with many from all walks of life and regardless of their background the key skills needed to be a good officer are common sense, the ability to learn, and learn from your mistakes, and a professional attitude. Top that off with a little bit of pride in yourself and you are on your way......

Professional Approach

A good professional approach to all things is important. None more so when we consider security implications.

ATTITUDE – STANDARDS – DRESS (A.S.D)

Your ATTITUDE says a lot about you. It subconsciously tells others how to treat you but it also determines in some respect your ability. A poor attitude equals a poor performance and a poor performance increases risk. We should all seek to implement a positive professional attitude in doing so we raise standards in the industry and create an atmosphere of increased confidence, not only within ourselves but we project it towards others whether that be colleagues or the public at large. Our ASD can be a defining factor of how we are treated by those around us.

When we talk of STANDARDS we are referring to not only the defined industry one but also the standard we set for ourselves. The way you implement your actions and the training you receive or seek out in order to be a professional individual all dictate the standard which you attain. The SIA license is one of entry level, therefore you should always be seeking to build on this foundation with training or further study. It is worth remembering that the license you hold is a individual one, it is yours to keep or lose.

I have heard many in this industry attempt to offset blame when poor drills have been implemented. It is true that you cannot train for every eventuality and study can only go so far. We are all very good at finger pointing and blaming others, and it is also true that an employer has a legal requirement to train its staff for the roles they undertake. However within this industry you need to be adaptable. An employer will as a cost saving measure only provide such training which is the legal minimum requirement. Therefore there is a lot of learning on the ground and as you go. It is human to make mistakes, we all do but if we don't learn from them we are destined to repeat them. So from now on prioritise assessing your own standard not the standards of others. Consider how you deal with incidents and dilemmas and seek out additional training which will improve how you operate.

It can often be a struggle to find specific training especially in the security industry. There has been an explosion in providers chasing the fast buck of providing level 2 & 3 license qualifications with advancement training being much harder to find it can also be a costly endeavour for minimal financial reward. If this is your view I can understand it but you must be able to assess your standard and ask yourself does it fit with the duties I perform and does it minimise the risk to me, my employer and the public at large.

One cost effective way to improve operational standards whilst reducing cost is to promote a de-briefing and assessment culture. You can improve standards and avoid dangerous repetition by doing so. Looking at how an incident or operation played out, what went well and what went wrong is a great learning tool. This should be standard operating procedure but it is often sadly overlooked. It has great value toward self improvement and the improvement of others whilst at the same time minimising future risk.

You have to own your own standards and then put them into practice. Nobody will do it for you. No matter what training you receive it is your decision whether to act on it or ignore it. Operate with pride and integrity. When it comes to standards take responsibility for there implementation.

When it comes to DRESS code nothing should need to be said we are all adults and we should know how to dress and we should know that how we dress tells others how we want to be treated. You MUST project the right image. If you do not then you do not instil trust or confidence in your abilities to others. This is not to say that you must look like you are on parade at all times although that would not be a bad thing. I have in the past worked with many who have turned up for work looking like they have ironed their shirt with a hedgehog. It is not just about a professional image its about taking pride in your own appearance. Therefore if you wear a uniform make sure it fits and is well maintained. I have seen on many occasions especially one particular large security company implementing the one size fits all policy when it comes to uniform. This may be fine if you are attending clown college but not if you want to be taken seriously.

I also personally have an issue with the polo shirt look. They lose their shape and soon become very untidy. I understand that you as an individual will have no input as to style of uniform issued and I often feel for those in that situation, but it is your duty to make the best of it. Make sure its clean ironed and well maintained. Wear the correct footwear for the task and look after them. Keep them clean, dry and polished.

If you operate in an environment where you are entrusted to wear your own clothes the same principles apply. It is not a fashion show, its about being smart and professional. I personally aim for the "grey man" look, which in simple terms is fitting in to my surroundings without overly drawing attention. If I need to wear a suit then its a dark one. I wear a white shirt and what I would refer to as a normal tie. Not eye-catching but not boringly repulsive and definitely not a kipper or pencil one. I also avoid the black suit, black tie, black shirt combination. The tight shirt look may show off your muscles but these two looks scream hey look at me I'm over here!!! Depending on your duties you may need to stand out but do it for the right reasons. If you work in nightclubs then the all black combination may be acceptable. It is not in my opinion however the correct form of security dress for outside of this environment.

Lifelong Learning

This is often a process that some avoid and many ignore. Our learning phase of existence begins at birth and remains throughout a persons life, whether we acknowledge this or not. From being a child we learn by being taught but also by watching and modelling others. We learnt to walk and talk by doing just that. As an adult one of the biggest hindrance to learning, or our willingness to learn is time. We live in a fast paced world where instant results and gratification is expected. In years gone by, before the advent of this culture, training and learning had more structure to it. The understanding of the need for extensive learning periods of theory and practical experience was appreciated and respected.

If we consider the modern approach to construction trades as an example, there was a time when tradesmen were revered in society, and those who wished to enter a trade would secure an apprenticeship with a respected, qualified and experienced trades person. Learn by modelling their actions and following their instruction increasing their own proficiency at each task. This would then be combined and enhanced by academic certification. This journey was not a rapid process, often taking six years of combined training in order to become qualified. After that period a newly qualified trades person would then progress to master his or her trade while continually learning new skills and approaches. This way of doing things was the norm and in some cases still is however you only have to look online to find many adverts for "Learn a trade" websites claiming to offer all the training needed and awarding the equivalent City & Guilds accreditation required for a commitment of only two weeks. The question you need to ask yourself is which type of trades person would you want working on your home.

The same thing can be said about many industries, and security is no exception. You cannot expect to learn everything you need to know by attending a one, three, fourteen or even a twenty one day course. These courses are a requirement to start work in the industry and offer the under pinning knowledge required, but they have to be accepted for that and not seen as the complete answer to your training requirements. As in all things you learn a skill slowly over time, at a pace that suits you. You learn the basics to take your first step and then you continually build on that skill and knowledge slowly gaining experience and wisdom. Increasing your professional skill set in order to equip you to safely and professionally deal with challenges.

Learning Principle

LEARNING STRUCTURE		
STEP 1	THEORY	**Studying & Academic Learning** (Research/book learning) (Training & Accreditation)
STEP 2	PRACTICAL	**Learn by doing** (Op experience)
STEP 3	MODELLING	**Seek out and model expert behaviour**
CONDITIONING (REPEAT STEPS 1 + 2 REGULARLY)		
STEP 4	MASTERY	**Worthy of being Modelled** (The Teacher)

Conditioning

"The process of carrying out repetitive action;
or learning in order to eventually create an automatic response"

Adding repetition and conditioning to a task whether that be reading a book repeatedly, continually reviewing or carrying out manual or academic activities over and over increases learning and recall and promotes fluidity of response. As they say practice often makes perfect.

By following and understanding the learning principle we are better placed to absorb and implement the best methods for increasing not only our knowledge of a subject but also practical excellence. The concept of repetition may feel to some as though it is an exercise in time wasting and pointless to do. On the contrary, by repeating actions it not only allows the review of material knowledge but with the addition of practical application will in turn create a new value or view point to the material, raise more questions and open up new avenues which would not be visible had the process not been undertaken. This repetition also increases fluidity of action, which enhances our Immediate Action response, making things and processes more automatic in nature and us less prone to hesitation.

By continually increasing your skills it not only benefits those around you. It provides you with the ability to do your job more safely for the public, your colleagues and yourself. It raises you up professionally, which in turn will raise others, and gets you ahead when it comes to your career. By the sheer nature of this industry and the risks involved it must be understood that in a worst case scenario, avoiding the principle of lifelong learning and accepting the belief that a short course provides all the skill required, the lack of additional training, knowledge, experience and wisdom could open the security officer up to prosecution.

It is not a sign of weakness to admit you do not know something but a sign of strength to accept your limitations and then seek the answer. Operations and duties evolve, law and common practices change and there are always new and innovative approaches being implemented.

It is often in our nature to get stuck in our ways, to become closed minded to change and sometimes fearful of doing things differently. However as referred to earlier our standards should always be something we attempt to build on and move forward with, with that in mind we have to accept that regardless of our individual intelligence there is always room for improvement.

> *"The capacity to learn is a gift,*
> *the ability to learn is a skill,*
> *the willingness to learn is a choice."*

> Brian Herbert

Self Learning

One benefit of living in this modern age is the access to information. It is often preferable to learn subjects in a structured environment where academic and practical teaching is provided and it must be emphasised that the academic path is the only way to secure the qualifications required to obtain a license to enter into security work but it must be pointed out that in order to improve quality of service an element of self learning is involved. It can be sometimes difficult to find specific training to compliment the sector in which you work, adequate training that offers advancement is often only provided to those in the public sector and provision of such training if it exists to private clients is often hard to find if at all. Online discussion forums, books and the internet all provide information at a click of a button but always fact check everything you read or discuss, search government and other respected websites and seek out publications from highly respected authors. If done correctly web search training, research and personal study should work to compliment any practical training received and improve both your personal and professional qualities.

Training Providers

Understanding the principles of learning and the process involved in order to achieve success, places an increased responsibility on the shoulders of those seeking to expand their training and qualifications. It is one thing expanding your knowledge and skill set through personal growth, experience and research. It is quite another finding those with the expertise worth modelling.

One modern phenomena of learning is the increase in train the trainer style courses. These courses being designed to teach candidates to tutor others, one of the largest growth sectors within the security industry is providing training to new industry entrants. The cash rewards for such has seen a mass increase in those wishing to provide that training.

"Tell me and I may forget,

teach me and I may remember,

Involve me and I learn."

Benjamin Franklyn

However when people undertake a course to teach a subject without first mastering it themselves the value of the training must be called into question. If you are paying to learn then you want to receive excellence from that trainer. If that trainer lacks the operational experience and can do little more than read from a book or give you a power point demonstration, then are they really capable of teaching a subject they have not mastered.

It is no longer wise to accept blindly that a provider is accredited to offer training, without understanding the criteria for obtaining that accreditation and whether it is robust enough in your eyes. It is only right that before you pay for, or decide on who should provide the training you seek, you investigate and obtain evidence of that trainers operational experience. Do your research and ask questions. A professional trainer which possesses a varied background and knowledge of the subject he is teaching will welcome this and it will hopefully drive those wishing to learn towards those able to teach.

Industry Success

First and foremost success within the industry starts with the individual. It is easy to point blame or deflect responsibility onto others. It is easy to play the "blame game" and for some this may feel like the norm especially in the security industry. It is correct that situations are reviewed and assessed in order to identify issues, but as an individual you must take ownership and responsibility for your actions and stand by them, accept when you are wrong and do all you can to increase your own abilities. In some sectors operational failure may only result in corporate financial loss. Within the security industry it can result in injury, loss of life and prosecution.

Philosophy

"A theory or attitude that acts as a guiding principle for behaviour"

Many say knowledge is power. That may be the case for many aspects of life but that alone does not equate to success. If having the information was all that is needed then expertise and reward would come easily. Life is not that simple, without a positive philosophy you cannot frame that knowledge or create success from it.

Your philosophy stems from your attitude and actions. A positive attitude combined with positive actions creates favourable results. When we talk of positivity in this context we are not referring to; nor suggesting that we need to be upbeat and smiling all day long, we are merely emphasising a results focussed frame of mind as the benefit it is.

No "How to guide" or instructional training course will work if it is in contradiction of your philosophy. If you focus on failure rather than success, or you become overwhelmed by the negative belief, then you will not get out of it what you expect or want.

Failing is a part of life, it just means you've done something. Some believe that doing nothing is often the best option, as by doing nothing in a situation or making no decisions being the safest approach. Inaction is often sometimes worse than the risk itself. Life is about risk and security is about managing that risk. The industry is just a natural progression from assessing risk as an individual, to assessing it on behalf of the wider community. The difference between the two is an important one to remember, as a security industry operator you are not only concerned with what's best for you but also what's best and safest for others.

Never be afraid to fail, as failure is often a prelude to success. All successful people throughout history have suffered failure at some point. It works to identify how not to do something in order that we can change our approach and find success. It provides experience which adds to our knowledge and creates new directions to try. A person who cannot, or will not adapt and learn from their own mistakes and those of others, will never know success.

CHAPTER TWO

Customer Service

"Quality in a service or product is not what you put into it.
It is what the customer gets out of it."

Peter Drucker

Customer Service is something that affects every business and individual regardless of the product or service supplied, good customer service promotes increased business and return customers. Whereas poor service can cost a company or individual contractor money. I have included this section in the book as you are a brand and should see yourself as such.

Role of Customer Service

Whether you operate as a paid representative of your employer, or are self employed providing security services on a freelance basis under short contract; offering excellent customer service increases your value as an individual. After all, providing an excellent service and meeting the needs of our customers is what security is all about.

We mentioned earlier the need for every sector worker to continually look at raising standards and how attitude and dress may dictate how others perceive you. It is the ASD approach that will demonstrate excellence in customer service. You are employed to promote a safe working environment and we do this by being knowledgeable, helpful, polite and respectful. Meeting our client and customer needs not only secures your position within an organisation but promotes the brand you represent, as well as your own personal one.

Customer Service attitude

The customer service attitude is one of helpful assistance. Having a good knowledge of both your role and the vision of your employer demonstrates a positive impression. But it must be emphasised that excellent customer service does not mean having all the answers. Things are ever changing in the business environment and you may only be working at this particular location for a short period, however this should not affect your level of response. You should always offer 100% whether you are a full-time employee, a short term contractor or even self employed on a day rate. You never know who you may meet, and a good level of service may open up networking and career opportunities which may otherwise be lost.

First impressions

These really do count, they say on meeting a person we form an initial impression within 7 – 10 seconds and this becomes embedded within 30 seconds. Once reached it is much harder to change their perception of you, so make it a good one.

Reputation

This is something slow to build but easy to destroy. We all seek a good reputation, whether that is at work or socially. As an individual or as a company brand a good reliable professional reputation is something we should all strive for.

Understanding your customers

Every customer, client and individual has needs, whether this be an access issue for somebody with a disability, information or assistance or a safety/security concern. From carrying out an assessment and impact study in order to minimise risk to our customers; to how we interact with them all falls under the customer service umbrella. Approach the situation as if you were your customer: consider what they may need, the difficulties they may have and what positive outcomes can be achieved.

Delivering Excellence

Maintaining and raising standards allows us to provide excellence in customer service and create a good first impression with all those you come in contact with. It puts others at ease, promotes mutual respect and admiration, increasing confidence in you in the minds of those you meet.

You should by now be considering the benefits of customer service. Not only does it make your working environment more pleasant and promote a positive attitude, it also facilitates the element of minimising risk, which is the key function of security. When we learn to approach situations by thinking of the needs of the client, assessing difficulties and providing outcomes, we are being proactive rather than reactive. This makes our role much smoother to implement.

Communication

Is the key to excellent customer service. In fact it is key to all aspects of life. If you are unable to communicate effectively then you will most certainly be unable to assist others or seek assistance yourself.

> *"Communication is a skill that you can learn.*
> *It's like riding a bicycle or typing. If you are willing to work at it,*
> *you can rapidly improve the quality of every part of your life."*

> Brian Tracy

We tend to view communication as a simple vocal process offering a statement or question and then expecting a response. However it is often much deeper. It is not just what you say it's how you say it. Your tone and body language all plays a part in how your message is received, after all 55% of our communication is believed to be non verbal, consisting of facial expression, gesture and posture. Therefore if you want to be understood you need to speak clearly, convey positive body language by making eye contact, utilising a correct facial expression in relation to the information you wish to pass Try to avoid poor posture and fidgeting. You cannot promote confident outcomes if you are looking down with your hands in your pockets.

> *"The single biggest problem in communication is*
> *the illusion that it has taken place."*

> George Bernard Shaw

Improving quality

The needs and expectations of your customers are often subject to change. You must continually reassess the service you offer and compare it with that of your competitors. It is vital that regular reviews take place and feedback is sought. It is imperative that you play your part, not only as a means of self improvement but to continually raise the standard of service within the industry.

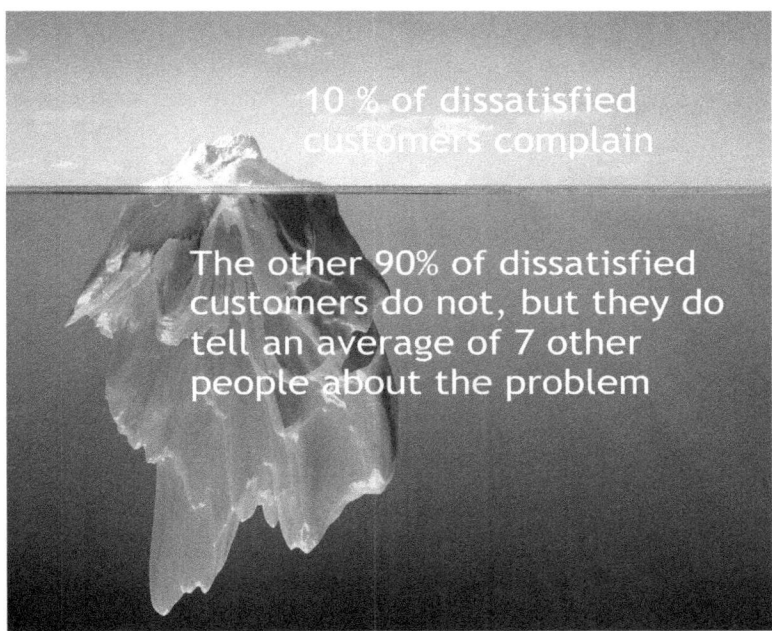

10 % of dissatisfied customers complain

The other 90% of dissatisfied customers do not, but they do tell an average of 7 other people about the problem

Dealing with difficult situations

When a difficult situation manifests itself in the form of a simple complaint, even though complaints are seen as a negative thing they should be used to promote positive change. It allows methods to be assessed, problems to be solved and change implemented.

If you can demonstrate empathy and understanding towards the aggrieved you can often calm down a difficult situation. If you fail to take their concerns seriously then the situation can quickly escalate towards hostility. It is your duty to listen and attempt to resolve the situation calmly and professionally, remain in control and not take things personally.

You need to be fully aware of your companies policies and relay accurate information. This section deals solely with difficulties in the form of problems and complaints, we will cover the escalation of hostility and possible breach of the peace outcomes in relation to proportionate legal response in further chapters. If you implement a good customer service ethos into your basic situation response it can often diffuse things. It should be viewed as step one in a process. If you follow basic steps and a situation still deteriorates you can quickly reassess and adapt your approach and justify your actions in doing so.

> *"Your most unhappy customers are your greatest*
> *source of learning."*
>
> Bill Gates

Problem solving

We can all benefit by increasing our problem solving skills, as we all encounter problems of varying degree on a daily basis. It would be wonderful to have the ability to solve any issue which presents itself with ease and little effort. Unfortunately this is rarely the case, problems are in themselves often complex.

The goal of problem solving involves setting out the "objective" of what needs to be achieved. This may be assessing the situation then asking yourself can this problem be avoided, if the answer is yes then you change your strategy and the problem is no more. If on assessment you decide it is not possible to avoid it then you need to deal with it.

The key is to identify and understand the problem then seek the solution, make a decision and implement your chosen course of action then re-assess and monitor to establish whether the problem still exists. The situation will now hopefully be solved. If not we run through our goals and objectives again changing the process of our action and implementation. Problem solving is an excellent way to gain knowledge and improve skill.

Boosting business

Excellence in customer service has two brand benefits. It promotes a positive response for your employer, increasing your employability and securing your position within the corporation but it also increases awareness of your personal professional brand. The value of this should not be underestimated. It is as equally important whether self-employed or permanent staff.

Thoughts

All the above points are valid and should be remembered. I have worked for many companies both large and small, as a member of staff as well as on a consultancy basis. I have found that the larger a company the more inclined they seem to be to put all employees on some form of customer service course during their induction. Unfortunately it often comes across more as a box ticking exercise rather than a useful aid for employment. To me it is the type of training which should actually be unnecessary for those which have common sense. It seems to be training which years ago would not have been considered. This is not because we have strived forward now in our learning and implementation but because to get a job you were expected to understand it already. I have sat in rooms for days listening with others to the proud company representative giving their take on customer service, using all the company buzzwords and positive jargon where 50% of the listening audience takes no part in the discussion and absorbs nothing from the experience, either because they are not interested or due to language barriers do not understand what is being said. They all sit politely and at the end of the course receive a certificate of attendance and sometimes get their photo in the company newsletter. Still oblivious to what had just transpired, return to work with the same lack of customer service skill they possessed prior to this exercise. The only purpose being served here is it shows the company as ticking the box in offering staff development training. It falsely shows the company as being a positive role model in the modern age. The company director, which then pays an accreditation body for membership, gets to attend an awards dinners, where they receive their compliance certificate and get their photo taken to place yet again in the company news letter. The cycle then continues year on year but on the ground nothing actually changes. This is a very cynical view I will grant you but I can only speak from what I observe. If you approach your work and all you do as a process of knowing your job, what is required of you, helping others and treating others with respect the same way you wish to be treated, and you have a helpful problem solving nature always considering the needs of your customers and clients, then as far as I'm concerned you understand customer service. This is an issue of common sense. Unfortunately all the power point presentations in the world cannot teach that.

CHAPTER THREE

Policing & Protective Services

"The Police are the public and the public are the Police;
The Police being only members of the public who are paid to
give full time attention to duties which are incumbent on
every citizen in the interests of community
welfare and existence"

- Sir Robert Peel

(1788 – 1850)

The duties and implementation of security services is often controlled by the policies and requirements put in place by our employers or clients. However the above quote although relating to the principle of policing serves to remind us of the nature of security, and the basic principles of those that should be working in this industry. Things may have moved on since the times of Sir Robert Peel but our need to help others should still exist. Albeit a reference to policing, it highlights an ethical standard which should be strong throughout law enforcement, public protection and indeed society.

The purpose of security is to promote a safe environment for ourselves and others. We accomplish this by policing the venue, site or area to which we are assigned, operating often as a first point of contact for visitors. We are looked to in order to provide assistance and guidance in emergency situations. It cannot be stressed enough how vital the role can be to the smooth running of any business.

More and more is being asked of the industry, new challenges and threats are posed daily. In order to meet these demands the industry has to provide a highly skilled adaptable workforce, equipped and trained to meet these needs. Understanding not only your trade but the importance of your commitment is vital.

Security is a protective service, one that should compliment not only the brand and public it is employed to protect, but also all the outside agencies it comes into contact with. By promoting and increasing professional and ethical standards the sector will rise to meet the challenges of the 21st century.

With increasing constraint on the public purse the security industry is being looked at in some regard in order to provide services which were seen in the past as the sole provision of government agencies. This consideration does prompt a lot of debate and concern amongst many in society. Understanding how to deal with incidents impartially, professionally and with confidence, whilst at the same time knowing the law in relation to not only your own actions but also in relation to the incident you are involved in is of paramount importance. Having the skills, and being capable and qualified to operate within acceptable guidelines to preserve evidence and crime scenes, and to obtain witness accounts and details, not only speeds up the time a responding police officer has to be involved but helps to maintain continuity of evidence and secures a conviction. All this will ultimately help to promote the smooth investigation of any offence or incident, freeing up all concerned to move on to the next task sooner. It is only by mastering this could the private sector offer real support to other agencies and complement them. This has to be be a priority for all in the industry. The ability to compliment law enforcement in your own operational service should be mastered before any company or individual even considers offering any service under contract which are currently provided by the public sector. Addressing the complimentary issue also benefits the brand of the company employing the security service due to their professionalism reflecting well on the employer, increasing the productivity and success of their operational objective, reducing the risk of prosecution for the security operator. Companies and individuals must tick these boxes if they want to be taken seriously and be considered for such contracts.

Consider the venue or location in which you work. Possibly it is a busy place like a shopping mall, bar or vibrant commercial enterprise. You need to consider staffing, individual visitors and capacity. If it is a retail or leisure venue you may have numbers equivalent to a small town passing through your doors on a daily basis. You therefore have to consider the safety and assistance needs of all that enter.

At the other end of the spectrum, your role may be more solitary, working at a vacant site or a location with limited or restricted public access. This may decrease some risk but raise others, as differing sites prompt differing challenges. I have worked at some of the busiest locations in the country and also some of the quietest. You would assume that complacency within a security team/detail stems from a quiet environment where little happens, whereas a busy site keeps you on your toes. This can be true, but unfortunately complacency can often creep in within both environments if a constant level of stimulus is maintained.

We are all capable of zoning out whether alone or in a room filled with people. For this reason professional security details rotate personnel in order to promote a variety in stimulus whenever possible. It is well advised that any officer pays attention to the risk of complacency, creating variety or mental challenges in order to combat it in ones own mind decreases the risk of a complacency error occurring.

As a protective services provider you are employed to protect people and property by minimising risk, assessing threat and implementation of contingency planning. This cannot be avoided, patrolling without considering threat, pre-planning and assessment of possible actions and out-comes puts you and others at risk. Not just from a safety prospective but from a legal one, flying blind and declaring ignorance is no defence for failure.

Role & Responsibilities

– To continually minimise risk whilst promoting a safe environment.

This industry is a diverse one, regardless of the specific duties of your contract the above role definition is your primary objective.

Under the umbrella of your primary role includes:

Customer Service Advisor

By implementing an active customer service policy and by doing so assisting others you are often pre-empting many issues and concerns from arising. Having an awareness of your clients/employers vision and objective promotes your value within that environment increasing a positive response for both you and your clients brand.

- Remember you are a brand in your own right
- Create a positive image
- Promote confidence

Policing

Providing security services within a venue means you are policing that venue with a remit to reduce/prevent crime and anti-social behaviour and to intervene in order to not only enforce company policy (providing it is lawful) but to protect people and property.

Contingency Planning

By risk assessing duties and considering possible outcomes we can consider avoidance measures in order to in some cases eliminate risk or reduce the chance of occurrence. It also allows you to think of measures to implement should this action occur, not only to reduce the risk of repetition but to act safely in order to bring any incident or dilemma to conclusion. For instance by directing foot traffic away from danger or conning of an area of car park or private highway due to congestion or an (RTC) Road Traffic Collision you are implementing contingency planning. This topic will be covered in greater detail in further chapters.

- Look at the environment in which you work and consider possible threat.
- Consider your Immediate Action Drill (IAD) = Response to events

Fire Marshalling

Mustering others and implementing fire precautions is a good example of contingency planning, knowing what to do in the event of a fire alarm activation is your responsibility .

First Aid

You should be, or aim to be with further training a qualified first aider or advanced first responder and should consider obtaining First Person on Scene (FPOS) medical training or Medical Intervention in Remote Areas (MIRA) qualifications. Any first aid training or experience is invaluable. I must at this point mention something which I find very annoying and unfortunately have experienced. If you work in an environment where you are not presently confident or trained to deal with medical emergencies don't ignore them. Attend if operationally possible and offer assistance, if just to reassure the casualty or assist the medic in attendance, or even to update those responding. In an emergency everyone has a part to play, luckily this avoidance is a rare occurrence but to even happen once in an environment with staff a plenty, there is no excuse.

These are just a few of the roles carried out by your average security officer. At the end of this book there is a selection of actual case studies involving some of the above duties demonstrating the importance of having a wide ranging skill set. All these duties promote a safe environment and therefore you as a security professional should embrace them. It is often those that say I'm security and that's what I do that don't even know how to provide a basic level of service. What they mean to say is I stand around doing very little projecting the illusion of security and nothing more.

Remember

- If you have concerns about operational implementation highlight them.

Never be afraid to ask questions and promote discussion, you may highlight something that warrants consideration. A good team environment will value your input, and it is wiser to do so before rather than after the fact for obvious reasons.

Responsibilities

- To familiarise yourself with the needs and objectives of your employer.
- To minimise risk and promote a safe environment.
- Promote an atmosphere of communication.
- Pre-deployment & Incident de-briefing.
- Identify threat/risk and be able to implement countermeasures.
- Understand the law which governs your actions

Teamwork

Teamwork is paramount in any job. A team player promotes a positive atmosphere and facilitates the smooth implementation of objectives. Whether you work in a small or large team each member has their value.

"I can do things you cannot,
you can do things I cannot;
together we can do great things."

Mother Teresa

We all possess differing strengths and weaknesses and a good team works well by promoting this diversity especially when it comes to understanding the objective. From pre-deployment briefing to dealing with incidents everyone's viewpoint is valid and the ability to pull together as a team can be the deciding factor in whether a situation deteriorates out of control or is pulled in the direction of success.

"Everybody is a genius. But if you judge a fish
by its ability to climb a tree it will live its whole
life believing that it is stupid."

Albert Einstein

(FPOS) First Person on Scene (Incident)

The FPOS principle is a control measure put in place when dealing with an on-site incident or dilemma, etiquette dictates that the first in attendance is the primary officer taking the lead in moving the situation forward. This creates smoother fluidity to the response. The first on scene can then brief and instruct others as they arrive. Having multiple officers talking over each other or dealing without structured communication can lead to things being overlooked and mistakes being made. Failing to do so can often make situations you are attempting to prevent come to fruition.

However it must be remembered by the FPOS that if they find themselves unable for any reasons to confidently deal with the situation, or in some circumstances the person they are dealing with becomes hostile toward them, they should step back and surrender control of the incident to others. Doing so is not a sign of weakness or failure it is a reassessment of the situation and the implementation of a new approach.

Patrol Equipment

Whether you provide all your own kit and equipment or if that responsibility is shared by your employer, it is still down to you to respect and maintain it. Confirm that everything is in working order prior to your start of duty, and report / replace all faulty items as soon as possible. If you are proactive in your approach you will be on your feet for long periods therefore it cannot be stressed enough the importance of wearing the correct footwear. Shoes should be practical, comfortable and fit for purpose, well made, a good fit and professionally polished. It is wise however depending on style and type to remember to break them in before you use them to patrol, many forget this and suffer the consequences.

You should always remember to dress for your environment, whether indoors or outdoors. If you're thinking about being hot or cold you are not thinking about doing your job effectively.

- Professional Footwear
- Professional Dress (smart attire)
- Weather suitable clothing
- Pocket book & pen
- Radio/Communications equipment

Pocket Book

Every officer working in security should carry a pocket book. This is not a notepad, it is a legal document and subject to court summons. It is a useful referral guide whilst giving evidence. A pocket book is a positive tool used to record your real time operational duties. The content should be incident specific holding the details of what has occurred and at what time. It holds the facts of the incident and the actions of you and others during that period. It must not contain opinion or speculation. Its purpose is to collate accurate information whilst it is still fresh, and should be filled out as soon as practicable to do so. It is a valuable asset for noting down witness accounts and contact details. A pocket book should be of sturdy construction, each page lined and numbered ideally with a margin on the left which you use to write the relevant time.

One excellent point to consider, especially if you think you don't need to carry one, or if you do that you can omit details because you have a can't be bothered attitude. In doing so you are taking a gamble, a risk which may return to haunt you further down the line. If 12 months later you get summoned to give evidence in court in relation to an old incident, you now have the worry of struggling to recall events from that period. In a case such as this having a pocket book containing the details and actions from the time would be invaluable during any prosecution or cross examination.

Example

Time and reference	
	22nd April 2015 start duty at (location) (Time)
0800	Begin patrol (assigned area/duties)
1014	Approached by customer alledging there was a verbal altercation
	taking place in the carpark only discription – 2x white males
	requested cctv obs made way to location, area checked
	thoroughly and canvassed nothing found – confirmed with cctv
1035	Stood down – No further action returned to patrol

Remember

- Record each days start of duty date time and location of employment
- All entries must be a narrative of the event, but may include drawings and sketch plans
- It is a legal document to be used in court to recall the event, it must be written in clear English and may be scrutinised by a judge, solicitor or barrister.
- Entries need to be made in chronological order as soon as it is practicable to do so.
- Use only black ink

- If a line is inadvertently missed a line should be drawn through it and marked "omitted in error" and initialled by the officer
- If a page is missed in error a diagonal line should be drawn through it and the above process repeated.
- Every entry should start with the time and location
- Record details, descriptions, names addresses of witness's
- If anyone refuses to give witness details (as is their right) record "details refused"

Etiquette

Take responsibility for yourself and the kit you use. Look professional and make sure your clothes are clean, pressed and fit for purpose. When it comes to radios, there is a belt clip for a reason, it goes on your belt not in your pocket as that serves no purpose, nor hooked or clipped to your trouser pocket as it will fall when you run. It also has an earpiece connector on it which should be used. An earpiece is a very practical piece of kit allowing communications to be sent more securely, as passers by do not need to hear what's being said, especially if its about them. If working in a noisy environment it means you can hear what's going on. Using this approach also means you consistently have both hands free but that is not an excuse to put them in your pockets.

This also seems an opportune moment to discuss mobile phones. When working a mobile phone should only be used as an emergency communication device. To call 999 or to use in the event your radio goes down. If there is no emergency it should be away. I could at this point stop typing get in my car and drive 5 minutes down the road to a location with security and I bet I will find one of them leant against the wall looking down at their phone. I am also pretty sure that you could do the same. What you need to remember is those that do this are not only stealing a wage from their employer but more importantly they are not being observant and when people stop being observant bad things can, and often do happen. So think on, could you live with yourself if one of your colleagues got stabbed while you were playing candy crush, and how would you justify that when they spin the cameras back to show the offender walked straight by you.

CHAPTER FOUR

Radio Communications & CCTV Support

"The two words, information and communication
are often used interchangeably,
but they signify quite different things.
Information is giving out; communication is getting through."

Sydney J. Harris

Radio Communications

Communication equipment and the ability to use it correctly is vital to the smooth implementation of any security operation. It allows the relay of messages and important information over distance, the passing of current situation updates and the ability to summon assistance in the form of additional officers or to contact CCTV control to re-task cameras to your location. Understanding radio procedure is a key aspect not only to facilitate the ability to work but also as a safety concern in an emergency. However with all things this skill sometimes takes time and has to be learnt. To some it is the most natural of exercises but others find it hard to master. If you are not confident on the radio and are concerned never be afraid to ask others (at a later time in person) how your transmission came across. As with all things accept any constructive criticism in the manner it was intended. Remember, especially if you are new to the industry, the ability to use a radio correctly is vital to your safety and well being at work.

As stated earlier using an earpiece and microphone is recommended over a hand held radio device, not only is this a benefit in practical operation it also reduces the risk of many common mistakes, such as holding the radio too close to your mouth, which can result in the transmission being garbled or holding it at arms length so no one can hear you. Or even some, who start relaying their message immediately on hitting the (PTT)

Push To Talk button, which results in the start of your message being missed, these offenders do exist.

Follow these basic principles

- PPS Press Pause Speak
- Accurate (pass relevant information only)
- Brief (Short and to the point)
- Clear (Vocabulary/Pitch/Tone of voice)

The Phonetic Alphabet

The NATO phonetic alphabet is used by the military, emergency services and the private security industry as a tool for transmitting information in a clear understandable manner.

A	ALPHA	N	NOVEMBER
B	BRAVO	O	OSCAR
C	CHARLIE	P	PAPA
D	DELTA	Q	QUEBEC
E	ECHO	R	ROMEO
F	FOXTROT	S	SIERRA
G	GOLF	T	TANGO
H	HOTEL	U	UNIFORM
I	INDIA	V	VICTOR
J	JULIET	W	WHISKEY
K	KILO	X	XRAY
L	LIMA	Y	YANKIE
M	MIKE	Z	ZULU

Whether passing a vehicle registration over the radio net or spelling out a misunderstood word this alphabet reduces confusion and minimises the risk of misinformation being passed.

One thing to remember, and I have heard this time and time again on the net, a colleague is passing details using this alphabet. Mid transmission the air goes silent as the officer racks their brain for the corresponding word to the letter they wish to transmit. You should always aim to use the above system, practice and learn it, but if by accident you say Zorro instead of Zulu for 'z' its not the end of the world. So don't panic, depending on the word you use (providing it is not offensive) it may raise a smile amongst your team but it still serves the same purpose.

Prohibited Language

This is one section which should need no explaining. However unfortunately either through laziness, poor skills or a lack of training, due to some of the things I have heard it does need to be mentioned. The radio network is a tool not a toy, foul or offensive language is not permitted. Nor is casual language such as using peoples names instead of call signs, nor is it to be used for arranging social activities. Using words like bomb, explosive or terrorist over an open radio net is also not permitted for obvious reasons, especially if you work in a public facing customer environment. I remember one particular instance walking through a department store with a colleague and over the radio came the message "a member of staff thinks she's found a bomb". Luckily I had an earpiece in but my colleague did not and in order for him to hear his radio the volume was cranked up and that transmission was heard by members of the public. Surprisingly it was a supervisor that transmitted that message and therefore they should have known better. Thankfully it was a false alarm but companies use incident codes to secure information for a reason. Learn them and use them. If you work for a company which doesn't have incident related codes then speak up and implement a system.

A simple colour code system.

CODE	
RED	FIRE
GREEN	MEDICAL
BLUE	DISORDER
BLACK	SUSPECT PACKAGE

Pro Words

These are words used to convey exact meaning allowing the radio operator to be understood without the need for repetition.

Example	Meaning
"OVER"	Signifies the end of transmission sentence, standing by for response.
"RECEIVED"	I have received/understood your last message
"SAY AGAIN"	Repeat your last
"OUT"	End of full transmission, no reply needed
"WAIT/STANDBY"	Indicates you are unable to reply at this time
"ETA"	Estimated time of arrival

Suspect Descriptions

When passing information over the radio to colleagues and especially to a control room in a request for observations regarding a suspect person/person of interest, use the following A to H system.

A= Age range of suspect with 5 years (e.g. 20 – 25 yrs)

B = Build (large/small/athletic etc.)

C = Colour (Clothing & Ethnicity)

D = Distinguishing marks

E = Elevation (Height)

F = Facial Features

G = Gait (Style of walk) + Gender

H = Hair (Colour & Length)

This is not a hard and fast descriptive process but is a good means of reference, as these are the details which are needed. However the environment in which you work as well as time constraints will be factors dictating how much detail you can pass.

Example:

You are on patrol at a large leisure complex with multiple staff and a CCTV control room. You witness someone acting suspiciously and monitor for yourself. Seeing nothing that warrants intervention at this time but something isn't right. You can at this point alert others and notify the control room to remotely monitor.

"(Call sign) to control .... send for control......., (Call sign) can you pick up on a white male at (location) large build.... 25 to 30 yrs ...short black hair...... 5'10 to 6' ..... wearing (Colour + type of clothing) ..... moving off now heading in the direction of (location)........ control to (Call sign) yes we have him, what's the issue? ..... (Call sign)..... to control request temporary observations on this gentleman due to suspicious activity on site....... Control to (Call sign) all received leave him with us OUT......"

Remember !!!!!

Always give locations, either your location if its incident specific or if observations are requested for subject that is on the move give the location and direction of travel, it gets assistance to you quicker if required and helps the control room obtain camera coverage. It has happened on more than one occasion when I have been venue based that a colleague has requested assistance, reported the details of the incident but failed to give a location until prompted by the control room, passing the location cuts down response times.

Depending on which field and industry you operate in will determine how strict radio procedure is but regardless of this you should have some standards of your own.

If you can transmit the information you are trying to pass clearly and be understood. And you can follow the basic principles of PPS (Push Pause Speak) and the ABC of information transmission. Then you have mastered the basics and with practice you will increase your confidence.

One final point to make. If you work on a contract basis you may work for many different companies or carry out multiple assignments each week. There is still no excuse not to know your call sign. I was once working in a staff role at a venue where an event was taking place and due to this an outside contract company was brought in, two of them being assigned to me. Whilst we were on duty their team leader came on the net calling one of the contract staff by call sign. As no one responded the two officers I was with began discussing between themselves whether it was one of them being called. Neither of which could remember their call sign. The debate continued and I asked why these details weren't recorded in your pocket books or at least write it on your hands, to which unsurprisingly they said they do not carry a book or even a pen. This demonstrates that even if you are there in body you are not effective if you fail on the basics. A radio is a lifeline and a tool to get the job done. If you don't understand the key elements to successfully doing your job then a company may as well save your salary and just put a Hi-Vis jacket on a dustbin.

CCTV Support

A good CCTV control room manned by professionals is vital in support of officers on the ground. They support you by passing information that may be relevant to the incident you are dealing with. They monitor you to minimise risk, to you and others. However the system only works well providing there is a good flow of communication between the control room and the officers on the ground. They have a panoramic view of any incident as it occurs and are often your link to the emergency services.

It may seem to the officers on the ground that a control room operators role is simple. Sitting on a chair watching a TV screen all day can sometimes create a them and us atmosphere. Depending on the location a control centre is a high pressure environment. Monitoring many screens; dealing with access control, logging incidents and data requests from government and law enforcement bodies and at the same time also be there for you when you need them. Therefore there should be a mutual respect between both parties. They have the pressure of multiple tasks and you as a patrol officer have the pressure of being in the line of fire so to speak.

The cameras may look down from above but they are not Gods. Even if some of the operators do have delusions of grandeur, a good control operator instructs you to carry out duties that have been passed down the line. However some of the poorer operators take this conduit task a step further and will try and direct you during an incident. The direction they should pass is one of assistance either bringing you up to speed on what may have occurred prior to your arrival, or as a means of providing real time updates. You can also seek opinion and advice from them but you must remember you are the officer on the ground and the operational decision making is yours. Never forget they can not hear what's being said and therefore if the incident is going on in real time in front of you then at that point the FPOS First person on Scene principle takes effect. This is where your training and your team working ability is tested. If a control room operator directs you to a course of action during an incident that you are uncomfortable with or an action you disagree with and you are happy to take the lead in directing a different course of action, do so providing it is lawful and you can justify it.

I have seen on thankfully only a few occasions officers carrying out instructions at an incident which have been decided by a control room operator which were unlawful. It cannot be stressed enough that the excuse of "I did it because I was told to" will not wash in a court of law. Not if the action was unlawful and as a security professional it is something you should be aware of. Ignorance is no defence. You are licensed and even though the licensing criteria is low, it is still your responsibility as an adult working in security to understand and justify all you do.

It must be emphasised that what has just been said does not detract from an employers or teams command and control structure. These command structures are in place for a reason. They allow for the smooth implementation of the objective and avoid confusion and anarchy. What I am trying to point out, that it is your responsibility as a human being working in this industry and for that matter any industry to act lawfully, knowing your trade craft and taking ownership of it and your actions. At the end of the day you and you alone are responsible for what you do. You have team leaders, supervisors and managers but what is often lacking is the confidence and ability to make sometimes split second decisions. Always seeking reassurance before action demonstrates a lack of adequate training.

CCTV Body Cameras

Wearable CCTV devices have in recent years become a popular tool not only for security personnel but also as a means of promoting safety for many workers. Whether you love the idea of wearing a body camera or loath it the practical benefit will see the use of them steadily increase.

Personally I am in two minds on the issue, on one hand they are extremely useful and practical, offering real time evidence gathering as a means to corroborate events. They may also be seen to work in a protective measure by alerting others to their use, discouraging those inclined to commit an offence. The only downside that does concern me and I must point out that this is a personal concern but not one which should be ignored, is the fact that as an operational tool the wearer needs to remember that they are responsible for maintaining this technology and securing the data held within, in a professional manner by adhering to data protection legislation. However the benefit of the use of this technology almost certainly out ways any concerns, and if respected and used correctly it can greatly assist in operational success. For those officers which routinely wear a camera as part of their duty then you must consider that in regards to the material you are the data controller, and as such must take all the appropriate technical measures against unlawful or unauthorised processing, loss or destruction of material.

General Operational Application

It is recommended that those who intend to use overt body worn CCTV devices to assist them in their duties visit the information Commissions website in order to obtain further legislative details and full guidelines on their implementation.

Visit : https://ico.org.uk/about-the-ico/

Advisable usage principles:

- Commence recording as soon as you are deployed to an incident, not on arrival.
- Record the incident from start to finish (continuity)
- Recordings should not be made of general duties
- Where possible announce the use of CCTV recording
- Material must be retained in accordance with the Data Protection Act 1998
- Material must be secure, only used or viewed by those with operational need
- Data held is open to Subject Access Request

Commencement of recording from the point of deployment rather than on arrival has many benefits, it may not be practicable or remembered on arrival depending on the possible overwhelming nature of the event. But it also promotes good audio and visual continuity. It can be used to demonstrate response times and can explain delays or distraction or interference whilst en-route.

When it comes to recording the incident, your camera needs to show the continuity of the event and your involvement without any breaks or gaps. There can be no discrepancy between your account of events and the evidence. Any gaps in footage damages the credibility of the evidence and may risk any conviction.

"Professional communication facilitates
a professional response"

P.J Mac

Incident Specific

This term is a key point to remember. When operating a body worn device providing security services the equipment needs to be used in an Incident specific manner. This means that you must not record randomly when on patrol. Remember the use of this equipment is for evidence gathering purposes not for entertainment. In some circumstances it could be seen as an invasion of privacy if it is used for any other reason. However a good point to remember, the more you record the more data you need to store and the more information you are responsible for, and as you should be aware any data held may become subject to an access request meaning you have to lawfully release the footage held on the device. Therefore only holding that material which is in relation to an incident will be beneficial to you and your time.

CHAPTER FIVE

Basic Law

"At his best man is the noblest of all animals;
separated from law and justice he is the worst."

Aristotle

Whether we like it or not the law governs our lives. It not only shapes society but the rule of law defines how we as individuals fit into that society. It instructs and guides us both in everyday life and at work. Therefore we should all have some understanding of the law. And when you work in a role where you are empowered to enforce company policy and prevent and deter crime, you cannot safely and professionally carry out your duties without it.

In this section we will discuss basic points of law, the differing types and touch on the legal process as a whole. This chapter has been added to aid discussion and to promote the understanding of this subjects importance in relation to your duties. It may seem daunting to some, but it is a vital topic when it comes to minimising risk. I must at this point emphasis I am not a lawyer. I have a layman's interest in this subject due to its importance in regard to providing effective service.

I have however studied Criminology and Criminal Justice and have extensive first hand operational experience. Regardless of this you should always read the relevant legislation and seek further study and clarification on any points raised prior to implementation. It is too often the case that we find ourselves at work listening to, and acting on advice from others when it comes to this subject. Whether that be from a colleague/manager or even from a law enforcement professional wading in with nothing more than their opinion.

Due to the complexity of this subject it is not possible within the confines of this book to tackle this subject in the depth with which it deserves. But if you take away an understanding of the importance of it, and as a result this promotes discussion and further learning then this chapter will have served its intended purpose.

Types of Law

Civil Law

"The system of law concerned with private relations between members of a community, rather than criminal, military or religious affairs"

For example, anything that involves a contract or agreement is ordered and controlled under civil law.

Criminal Law

"The body of law which is concerned with the punishment of offenders"

Oxford English Dictionary

A crime is an action or omission which constitutes an offence and is punishable by the law.

Criminal law, for the purposes of our role is the law which we are enforcing or mitigating against the risk of. However both laws are used to govern us in our actions and duties as citizens.

Laws are established by one of three routes:

Statute Law – These are laws which come into effect by acts of parliament

Common Law – Laws which become established over time as a result of society

Case Law – These are laws which come into effect as a result of legal precedent

We are not the police and do not possess police powers. We have no greater validation than any other citizen. However as a citizen we do hold the power to arrest for an indictable offence.

Indictable Offence

An indictable offence is considered as; a serious offence which can only be tried on indictment in Crown Court. They are offences which carry a possible 5 year prison term.

Crimes such as:

- Theft (Theft act 1968)
- Murder
- Manslaughter
- Fraud
- Assault (Offences Against the Person Act)
- Criminal Damage (Criminal Damage Act 1971)
- Burglary (Theft Act 1968)
- Robbery (Theft Act 1968)
- Drugs (Misuse of Drugs Act 1971)

Visit : www.legislation.gov.uk/browse

Theft

> *"A person is guilty of theft if he dishonestly appropriates property belonging to another with the intention of permanently depriving the other of it"*

Theft Act 1968 Chapter 60 section 1

There may be many mitigating factors to disprove the act of theft has taken place. However we are discussing this from the point of view of a security professional working at a entertainment venue or within a retail environment. All of which is considered privately owned property, allowing limited public access for the provision of the sale of goods or services.

For this type of venue leave to remain is granted by the owner or management of the site. It is the role of the employee to enforce conditions of entry as laid out in your policy document. Monitor those inside for safety and policy breaches.

In relation to theft in these locations you need clear evidence of the act and continuity in relation to observations of the offender. We will cover this in greater detail later in the chapter on retail security.

If we are referring to residence we mean private property with no lawful right of public access - namely a home. This type of building may have security for a multitude of reasons, possibly due to the profile of the owner or the value of assets within. Therefore in the case of this type of property, the fact it will be secured or should be and entry forced, whether by breaking and entering or knowingly trespassing in a part of a building and stealing or attempting to steal property belonging to another. They are committing the act of burglary.

Visit : www.legislation.gov.uk/ukpga/1968/60/contents

Burglary

Burglary is the illegal entry into a building or dwelling with the intent to commit a crime - namely theft.

Aggravated Burglary

Burglary in all forms falls under the Theft Act 1968 and as such is an indictable offence. The term aggravated burglary refers to a burglary in which the burglar commits the offence whilst having in his possession a weapon.

- **WEAPON**

- **IMITATION FIREARM**   **W.I.F.E**

- **FIREARM**

- **EXPLOSIVE**

Possession of includes:

a) On their person

b) In a location accessible to the offender (for instance by an entry point).

Robbery

"A person is guilty of this if he steals property, and immediately before or at the time of doing so and in order to do so, he uses force on any person or puts or seeks to put any person in fear of being then and there subject to force"

Robbery is also indictable and falls under the 1968 Theft Act.

Trespass

"The act of being upon, or entering, land or premises without the right to be there"

Trespass is a CIVIL OFFENCE and as such you have no powers to arrest for trespass. Please remember this. I have seen on countless occasions a security officer threatening to detain (Arrest) a person for trespass and call the police. This may be a good threat to make in order to scare off a trespasser but don't act on it because you may find yourself committing an arrestable offence. You advise them they are trespassing, this is your first duty. If they are ignorant of the fact they may leave voluntarily. If they do not then you reassess the situation. Why is this person refusing to leave? Are they now a threat? Do any of their actions fall under the remit of an indictable offence?

Aggravated Trespass

"Is the action of entering private property or land in order to intimidate, disrupt or obstruct those within from carrying out their lawful activities."

Aggravated trespass is a criminal offence, however not an Indictable one. It can only be enforced by a police officer or those acting in the presence of; and under instruction of a police officer.

With all things you need to implement a level of common sense. If a trespasser is in possession of a weapon and this is visible to you, trespass is the least of your concerns.

If he's waving a baseball bat or a knife for instance I would not be informing him he is trespassing. Or by their actions you have a strong belief that an indictable offence has either already been committed, namely assault or criminal damage or suspect it is imminent. This even includes offenders who inform you they are in possession of a weapon even without it being visible to you.

For those working in licensed premises there is a specific act of parliament that entitles agents of the company to withdraw any patrons leave to remain. The Licensing Act 2003 takes into account the use of the premises and allows for additional protection in the event of disorder.

Licensing Act 2003: Failure to leave licensed premises

Visit : www.legislation.gov.uk/ukpga/2003/17/contents

The Licensing Act 2003 - Chapter 17 / Part 7 / Section 143 covers duties of the licensee and their agents/Door Supervisors in relation to admission and ejection of persons from licensed premises.

1)   A person who is drunk or disorderly commits an offence if, without reasonable excuse-

a) Fails to leave relevant premises when requested by a constable or by a person to whom subsection (2) applies, or

b) he enters or attempts to enter relevant premises after a constable or a person to whom subsection (2) has requested him not to enter.

2)   This subsection applies -

a) To any person who works at the premises in a capacity, whether paid or unpaid which authorises him to make such a request.

b) In the case of licensed premises to -

       (i) The holder of a premises licence in respect of the premises, or

       (ii) The designated premises supervisor (if any) under such a licence,

c) In the case of premise in respect of which a club premises certificate has effect, to any member or officer of the club which holds the certificate who is present on the premises in a capacity which enables him to make such a request, and

d) In the case of premises which may be used for a permitted temporary activity by virtue of part 5, to the premises user in relation to the temporary event notice in question.

3)   A person guilty of an offence under subsection (1) is liable on summary conviction to a fine not exceeding level 1 on the standard scale.

4)   On being requested to do so by a person to whom subsection (2) applies, a constable must -

a) help to expel from relevant premises a person who is drunk or disorderly

b) help to prevent such a person from entering relevant premises

In simple terms the above gives you the right as a door supervisor or agent of the management to refuse admission or expel patrons if you believe them to be intoxicated. Or if they act in a disorderly manner.

A licensed venue will have a conditions of entry policy. When a member of the public gains entry to such it is on the condition that they accept this policy. Any breach of this policy could be viewed as disorderly conduct and their right to remain withdrawn. However it must be remembered that any entry conditions must be in line with the law, written in a informed manner, and known to all.

Breach of the Peace

This is a common law power of arrest, utilised in order as it would suggest; to prevent a breach of the peace. In as far as the security industry is concerned we are talking about the prevention of an indictable offence. However this is a very broad type of offence in itself and open to misinterpretation. A good study of case law would demonstrate the risks of arrest for this offence. When it comes to private security you must if using this power only do so to prevent an immediate threat to a breach of peace. For instance to prevent an action of criminality. Once a threat is no longer posed then arrest or detention must cease or the continued restriction of liberty could be considered unlawful and you risk a charge of false imprisonment. Putting this in raw terms, consider a situation where a physical altercation is about to erupt, intervention may be required to restrain and separate the parties. An indictable offence has not occurred as you have prevented it. The parties have both calmed and are now separated, no longer posing any immediate threat. Therefore what would be the justification for a continued restriction of liberty by holding or restraining one or more parties.

Criminal Damage

"A person who without lawful excuse destroys or damages any property belonging to another, intending to destroy or damage any such property or being reckless as to whether any such property would be destroyed or damaged shall be guilty of an offence"

Criminal Damage Act 1971 Chapter 48

As stated earlier criminal damage is an indictable offence and a security officer may arrest for this offence.

Assault

There may be many considerations regarding assault, whether the offence is aggravated i.e. a weapon is used. If it is premeditated, common assault, ABH or GBH. As far as we are concerned implement a bit of common sense. Any aggressive physical body contact could be considered as assault. Allow the investigating authorities to determine what particular charge should be laid on the offender.

Fraud

"Wrongful or criminal deception intended to result in financial or personal gain"

Fraud Act 2006

Fraud is one indictable offence, which by its nature is often a premeditated deception. Due to the many layers that may be involved it is sometimes hard to identify and as such often requires a great deal of investigation. In relation to the duties of a security officer it is something that you may come across quite often if you work in retail. Retail fraud is widespread with credit card fraud alone (according to the Centre for Retail research) costing the retail industry in the UK 85 Million pound in the year 2012/13. However it is rather something point of sale staff need to be aware of just as much as security personnel as they will be better placed to monitor and detect. It can sometimes be a grey area as to whether fraud in a retail environment has taken place. But if suspected CCTV and Store Detectives should be utilised in an evidence gathering role, details shared and compared with the police as part of the retail crime initiative. By its nature it is a deception and in doing so attempting to obtain goods or services. Therefore specialist training in fraud prevention should be undertaken by all officers working in high risk environments.

Public Order Act 1986

The Public Order Act was established to replace particular offences within common law. You as a security officer are not empowered to arrest for breaches. It can only be enforced by a police officer. If you feel that a public order offence has been or is in the process of being committed, and you feel that it warrants reporting and it is practicable then do so.

It is advisable to take note of this because speaking from experience I have been in a number of situations where a security officer has threatened to in their words "Bring em in, for "Public order" after hearing repeated foul or racially motivated language. Watching re-runs of the Bill or some other police drama may be fun but they are entertainment not training programmes. If you get your attitude to duty and legal knowledge from the TV you are going to come unstuck.

Visit : www.legislation.gov.uk/ukpga/1986/64/contents

Remember Think "Indictable offences"

Misuse of Drugs Act 1971

Possession of most controlled substances is an indictable offence and on conviction a person may receive up to 10 years imprisonment.

However sentencing may vary considerably depending on the quantity and grading of the controlled substance. For obvious reasons Class A would result in a longer sentence than class C. As with all offences it is advisable that you review the acts of parliament in order to understand it for yourself. When it comes to powers of arrest you need to be able to prove a reasonable belief that an indictable offence has been committed. And if you observe the possession, use or supply of a controlled substance (especially concerning class A or B) you have the right to arrest and secure the substance and call the police.

You have the right to secure in order to:

- Deliver the substance into the custody of a person lawfully entitled to take it
- Prevent the commitment or continued commitment of the offence

If it looks like a controlled substance and you have reasonable suspicion that an offence has been committed you have the right to intervene.

Data Protection Act 1998

It is the duty of all to protect and promote the security of information held. To only hold and have access to that information which is relevant and necessary. And to securely keep data which is freely given to you by others. Any information held must be done in compliance with the Data Protection Act 1998.

visit : www.legislation.gov.uk/ukpga/1998/29/contents

For those working in a security patrol officer capacity this would include all details freely given and held in your pocket book. Any witness statements and investigative material and any audio or video evidence obtained. All material must only be kept for the period for which it is necessary to do so. That which is considered used or no longer needed must be securely destroyed.

Subject Access Request

In accordance with freedom of information and the Data Protection Act, any material held on an individual, either in document, video or audio format may be subject to release on request by that individual or individuals. This is referred to as a Subject Access Request. Any request received in writing and in accordance with the DPA1998 should be actioned and made available within 40 days of receipt of that request. A charge of up to £10 is often used as a permissible charge to administer. However in some cases there may be other legal barriers to the release of the data. It is the responsibility of the data controller (person holding the data) to understand the law and their legal obligations.

Powers to Search a Person

The simple and straight forward answer to this is:

You have no powers to search any person without their consent !!!!

It may be a condition of entry to a venue or of employment in a particular environment. Making someone aware of this condition gives them the option to accept or decline admission.

Searching a person can be a very intimidating experience and if not carried out in an empathetic manner can create a level of hostility, delaying the process and sometimes escalating the situation.

Any person working in the security industry whether they routinely carry out searches as a part of their employment, should be routinely aware of the process of carrying out a non intrusive search of a person. Focus should be made on encouraging those to be searched to empty out there pockets and bags as it reduces the risk of you suffering injury by routing through another persons possessions. It also reduces any claim that an item may have been planted. When we are considering search procedures we are doing so in a condition of entry application. When it comes to making an arrest the detainee should not be searched. This situation is completely different, and the detainee (person under arrest) merely held until the police arrive.

I remember being involved in a case where a customer had alleged her purse had been taken from her bag, she was obviously distraught over the incident and had reported it to venue security. She alleged that the girl next to where she was sat had taken it. I (as a security representative for the complex in which this venue was located) was despatched to oversee and offer assistance. The venue door staff had already taken the alleged perpetrator into their office and was supervising her until my arrival. The suspect was fully compliant at this time. On arrival I firstly asked the manager if there was any CCTV of the incident, unfortunately there wasn't. I was then introduced to the alleged victim, she was extremely angry at what had occurred and demanded that I search the suspect. I informed her that it was not legally possible to do so. I did say I can ask them to empty their pockets, but any search of the person is reliant on them giving permission and would risk securing a prosecution. This did not go down well and the alleged victim stated "I work in security and search people all the time..... I'll do it, I'm allowed to". I asked where she worked and she said she does "the festivals", I did not get into the issue of compliance and the law at this point. I just obviously refused her request. It was at this point the ladies partner returned and to cut a long story short the misplaced purse was not lost or stolen but rather had been taken by her partner by mistake. It was the result of a communication issue rather than a crime. The alleged suspect rightly received an apology and the venue compensated their visit. The alleged victim was now in a state of embarrassment about it all. Details of all parties were logged and each went on their way. This incident was not perfect. It was just lucky that the accused person was extremely accommodating. But I highlighted this because if the alleged victim had in her anger forcibly searched a suspect that was at the time in my care, it would have been her risking arrest, and if she had found her purse during that search it may have jeopardised securing a conviction. I put the alleged victims determination to search down to her emotional state and desperation to find her property. But it acts as a reminder to all, you need to know the grounds and reasons why you may carry out particular actions in certain circumstances. You must know what is acceptable and legal and in what circumstances and at what time. The reasons as to why you can do some things and not others is controlled by the law. The fact she worked at festivals means she has experience of carrying out a condition of entry search of property and person. This is far from the reason she wanted this individual searched. And to encourage or forcibly search an alleged offender could easily be considered assault.

Use Of Force

The use of force should only be used to:

- To protect oneself

- To protect others
- To protect or prevent injury to the aggressor

P.L.A.N FOR SUCCESS

Is your use of force:

Proportionate to the "PERCIEVED" threat

Legal

Accountable - record your reasoning for your actions

Necessary - can you justify your actions and infringement of rights to a third party?

This is one subject I hope you are already extremely aware of. Your SIA license criteria training should have covered this in depth.

Key word & Questions

Reasonable:

Were your actions reasonable considering the incident and level of perceived threat?

Proportionate:

Assessing the threat as you see it. Were your actions in line with an accurate response in order to nullify that threat without being excessive?

Justifiable:

Can you justify your actions to others?

Hindsight is a wonderful thing. De-constructing your actions at a later date or on a debrief with others, especially when you are under the microscope, may seem like a vexing process. I for one am extremely guilty of over analysing my actions after the event. However this can be a valuable exercise to assess how we approach situations and how we can change or possibly do things differently next time should things happen again. For me, when I do look back and assess my actions during an incident my first consideration is to how I felt emotionally in regard to the threat. Different people may have totally different perceptions of how they felt regarding the threat level.

Consider this, picture yourself playing rugby. You're on a field with 29 other players... the play is moving away from you so you can watch as they chase the ball down the field. Suddenly play changes direction. The ball comes flying towards you and you catch it. Now all you can see is the opposing team of 15 giant men bearing down on you. The threat level has just increased and you have to react.

The above scenario demonstrates that even though there may be many involved it is down to you and your perception of an event which should dictate your actions and provide justification for your reasonable and proportionate response.

Powers of Arrest

You may after all you have read think non of this applies to me as I don't arrest people I detain them. Well if they volunteer their own detention, i.e. you ask them to remain and they fully comply then that's fine. But unless you work in a very amenable location I would expect that to be a rarity. If you are detaining somebody who chooses to leave and you are preventing them from doing so, then you are restricting their liberty and in doing so you are either placing them under lawful arrest or falsely imprisoning them.

Arrest : The restriction of liberty

Serious Organised Crime and Police Act 2005 (Section 24a)

1) Arrest without warrant: Other persons -

   a) anyone who is in the act of committing an indictable offence

   b) anyone whom he has reasonable grounds for suspecting to be committing an indictable offence

2) Where an indictable offence has been committed, a person other than a constable may arrest without warrant-

   a) anyone who is guilty of the offence

   b) Anyone whom he has reasonable grounds for suspecting to be guilty of it

3) But the power of summary arrest conferred by subsection (1) or (2) is exercisable only if -

   a) the person making the arrest has reasonable grounds for believing that for any of the reasons mentioned in subsection (4) it is necessary to arrest the person in question; and

   b) It appears to the person making the arrest that it is not reasonably practicable for a constable to make it instead

4) The reasons are to prevent the person in question -

   a) causing physical injury to himself or any other person

   b) suffering physical injury

   c) causing loss of, or damage to property or;

   d) making off before a constable can assume responsibility for him

   Section 25 of PACE (general arrest conditions) shall cease to have effect

Visit : www.legislation.gov.uk/ukpga/2005/15/section/110

When making an arrest for an indictable offence the following must be explained to the suspect.

- Who you are - identify yourself as a security officer, store detective etc. ...
- That you are arresting them
- The reason for the arrest

This not only complies with article 5 of the Human Rights Act 1998 in regard to the treatment of arrested persons. It proves continuity in your actions and helps to protect you legally should the suspect become aggressive in resisting.

Visit : www.legislation.gov.uk/ukpga/1998/42/schedule/1/part/I/chapter/4

You should also when making the arrest as soon as it is practicable to do so caution them.

The Caution

"You do not have to say anything, but it may harm your defence if you do not mention, when questioned anything you later rely on in court. Anything you do say may be used in evidence"

Many seem frightened of the concept of making an arrest and their liability in doing so. But your liability becomes greater in not doing so. You need to be able to prove continuity in your actions. Making your actions clear to those that you are detaining,   arrest allows for this. Remember if a suspect chooses to remain that is one thing. If you are stopping them from leaving its a restriction of liberty and arrest is the only lawful restriction of that liberty.

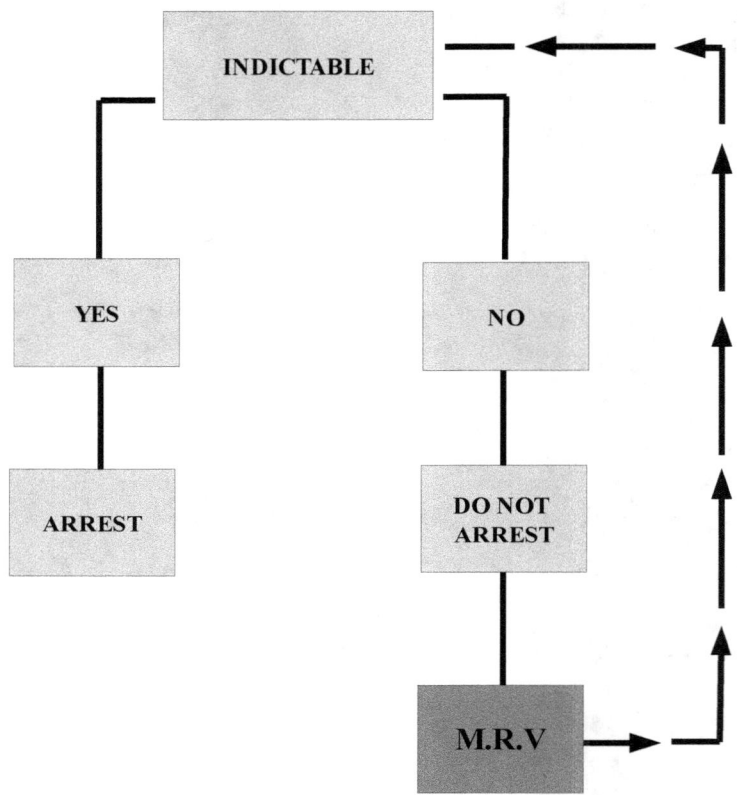

M.R.V (Monitor Reassessment Variables)

This is the process of continued monitoring of the event or situation and then reassessing it. For instance a person may be committing an offence which could be seen as a public order concern, possibly using foul or abusive language (Not an Indictable offence). During this the assailant in a rage damages property which does not belong to them. The reassessment now tells you the indictable offence of criminal damage has been committed. Or are they becoming increasingly aggressive bordering on violence. In either case you may consider arrest.

The point here is not to focus on the broad elements of unacceptable behaviour and always intervene in an attempt to de-escalate every situation but arrest only for the correct and permissible reason.

Having worked in environments where the management team would promote the mantra of "we do not arrest, we detain" in an attempt to separate the two issues. They are not, arrest is a form of detention, but so is false imprisonment. To make the detention of another legal it must involve and fall within the framework of a lawful arrest. Knowing this and absorbing the fact that any restriction of liberty, which is any situation where one person is not allowing another to leave and go about their business must be considered and treated as a lawful arrest. Failing to understand this may see the person forcibly restricting another's liberty, facing prosecution and risking their own safety. To define it differently is extremely dangerous.

It is also a general misconception that once you make a lawful arrest you have to log every word the suspect says, and by avoiding doing so reduces your paperwork. This is not the case. Whether under arrest or not, if a suspect makes an admission, or speaks in relation to the incident then common sense dictates you make a note of it in your pocket book and add it to your statement. You do not need to note down every word out of their mouths. Another thing to remember is, you are not there to conduct an interview. You are dealing with the facts as they are laid out to you. Leave the interviews for the police.

What you have just read is intended as an overview of some of the elements involved with regard to the implementation of your duties. Not only to your employer but especially to yourself and society. This is not to say you need to be a lawyer, what you need is a basic understanding and willingness to absorb as much legal knowledge as possible but above all have the confidence to act professionally. Take ownership of your decisions and implement them. This section would need to be a book of many volumes if it did cover all the aspects of law which may affect you. The chapter alone cannot hold every piece of useful information required, it combines legal knowledge and personal opinion, but does link to some relevant legislation and should increase your knowledge, professional practice and safety on the job promoting discussion and deeper investigation. Knowing what offences you can and cannot arrest for minimises risk and promotes a lawful approach. Never be frightened to question things and look things up for yourself. As they say knowledge is power and wisdom in practice will reduce your own personal risk, raise your standard and protect you against prosecution, promoting successful operational outcomes.

Civil Law

This section has been added mostly due to experience. The line between civil and criminal offences and indeed indictable offences can often seem blurred especially when you are in an emotionally charged situation. The risk of this confusion can have a profound effect on the legality of any action. Therefore for this purpose we will merely define it in an attempt to understand the difference between these types of law in order to be in a better place to advise, rather than act incorrectly.

Let me point out one thing early on:

You cannot arrest or threaten arrest for any breach of civil law.

Any location in which you work that provides goods or services to the public in a point of sale capacity has to conform to civil legislation, one of which is the sale of goods act. For the purposes of allowing it to be understood more easily and differentiated from other forms, we will consider a civil offence to be any offence in which it could be deemed a breach of contract between two parties. For instance if you purchase a product from a shop or other business and the item becomes faulty or broken then you have the right as a consumer to return the goods. Many places will happily refund or replace immediately. However if this is a large store that is part of a chain sometimes their policy may require the involvement of head office. The moment you present yourself in the store they may be unwilling to act without head office approval. In that case all they need to do is provide the customer with details of the process and contact information. It is understandable that with some items investigations need to be carried out in order to establish whether the product is faulty or has been damaged or misused by the purchaser. If you work in such an environment where you may be called to a store or business within a complex or centre, you are only there to prevent a breach of the peace or an indictable offence being committed. If the situation becomes aggressive you reassess and act accordingly. Being able to empathise and assist both the shop assistant or manager who may be following policy and the customer often de-escalates the situation reducing hostility. It is not your job to take sides it is your job to maintain a safe environment. I have been in many situations where an irate customer in a store is screaming "I know my rights" and becoming more and more aggressive and intimidatory towards the staff. And yes you may know your rights, but it is not your rights you are angry about at this point. It is the speed at which the dispute is being dealt with and instant gratification may not be possible.

A security officer in this situation must remember that they are not there to voice their opinion on the situation nor the item, saying it looks shoddy or you have purchased a similar item and it fell to pieces. Both are things I have heard come from the mouth of a security officer. If you do this you are breaching the rule of impartiality and could be seen to be assisting in some form of intimidation. It will also without doubt get you mentioned in all subsequent correspondence between the parties, with your comments being used by the purchaser to re-affirm their position, when in reality all you did was implant your opinion and speculation. If you have the knowledge to advise on points of law then do so if you are confident, but keep opinion to yourself.

CHAPTER SIX
Threat / Risk Assessment

"The first step in the risk management process
is to acknowledge the reality of risk.
Denial is a common tactic that substitutes deliberate ignorance
for thoughtful planning."

Charles Tramper

When you think of risk assessments you could be forgiven for picturing a boring man with a clipboard. But risk assessment is something we all do, and have been doing it all our lives with varying degree of success. Well if you are reading this then you have already had some success by the fact you are still alive.

From being a child right through to adulthood we consider what we either need, or want to accomplish and we assess the risks of doing so. If it is something new to us we may take greater notice of our need to consider the dangers and outcomes. However even in the most routine of activity like crossing the road we stop look listen then cross. We assess the traffic and minimise risk by crossing in time with and at the lights. Therefore as a duty of care to ourselves, our employers, customers and clients it is vitally important that we focus a great deal of attention on assessing and minimising risk. We do this by first of all considering our objectives and those of our employer in order to identify all threats posed.

Threat:

Any known credible action which aims to prevent or hinder the success of your objective.

Risk:

The consideration of factors which may or may not disrupt operational success.

In order to increase the chance of success and mitigate against the risk of failure we must implement assessment strategies, not only as a pre-deployment measure but as a continual means of operational assessment. Some threats and risks remain constant whereas others may present themselves as an unforeseen circumstance or as a result of our actions.

When it comes to assessing threat you must consider the operational objectives of your employers business, maybe you work for a pharmaceutical company which is being targeted by a particular group or threats have been sent to the director of the establishment. You may work in a retail environment where you sell particular products, increasing the chance of you being targeted for disruption by organisations promoting animal welfare. You may also receive threats from former company employees. The point is to consider the company and those which may intend to disrupt its operation. You have to also consider risks which occur as a result of the role or service provided by the employer. The building in which you operate the numbers of staff or visitors that attend and the facilities available to them.

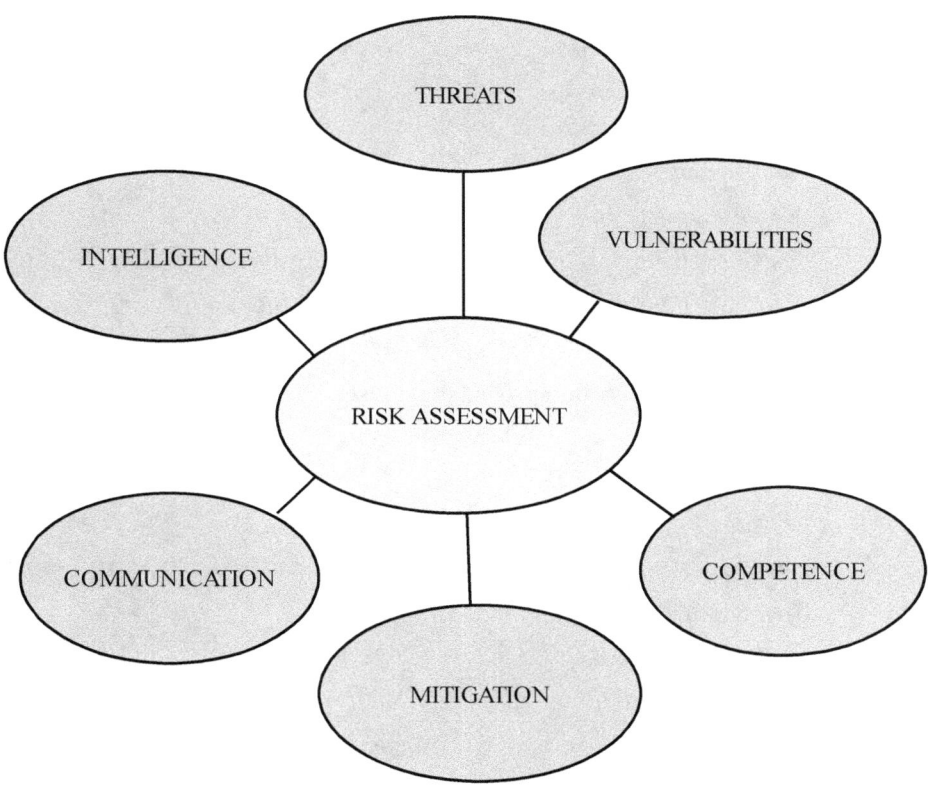

Your first priority working in a general security/policing role when considering risk is the risk to yourself. This does not mean that you are all that matters and it is okay to be selfish. What it means is by considering the risks to you regarding your role you can carry out your tasks in a safe manner. If you take unacceptable risks you become ineffective.

You must carry out pre-planning and pre-deployment briefings so you can be aware or make others aware of current threats, threat level and changes to environmental factors. Risk is often something that evolves and changes and we have to constantly re-evaluate in order to understand and counter it.

Type of Threat:

- Violence
- Criminal Damage
- To Life
- Blackmail
- Terrorism
- Postal (written or Suspicious package or I.E.D)

Remember all threats are credible until proved otherwise.

Type of Risk:

- Structure & Building fabric
- Staffing
- Access & Egress
- Deliveries
- Products – on site storage (valuable assets and Hazardous material)
- Crime (shoplifting, Criminal Damage & Disorder etc.)
- Medical Emergency
- Equipment malfunction/failure
- Postal
- Blackmail
- Violence & Threats to life
- Natural Disaster/Event
- Terrorism

If we consider a threat as credible until proved otherwise. Action to disrupt, damage or destroy life, or liberty and property which has been received by the company or one of its employees or agents either directly or by the use of intelligence gathering. Whereas risk considers not only the possibility of such actions, but all actions which are detrimental to the smooth operational success of your objective.

Considerations:

Structure and building fabric

Is the building structurally sound, is there damage to any internal fabric of the building. If so report it to the proper authority for repair.

Staffing

Is there sufficient staff to maintain an effective security presence. And is that staff competent and trained to operate effectively. Do non security staff have security awareness training and are all staff with full access vetted to work in that environment.

Access & Egress

Are sufficient controls in place to assist staff and visitors on entering and exiting. And can you monitor while on site. Are areas without access to the public or staff secure and are external doors, barriers and locks fit for purpose and operational.

Deliveries

Are deliveries logged prior to arrival, do you know who and what will be arriving and at what time. Do you check and sign in all delivery goods and operatives, and monitor their vehicles and movement on site.

On site product

Do you store valuable assets or hazardous material and are they fully secured and monitored in restricted access areas.

Crime

Do you actively minimise the risk of crime by monitoring, patrolling and deterring. Do you have the training to diffuse hostility, to make arrests and implement counter-measures.

Medical Emergency

Do you have first aid cover. This is a legal requirement, how experienced and equipped is it. What medical kit do you possess and where is it kept. Do you know how to use it or assist in the use of it. Do you know the post code location of the site or venue you are working as the 999 dispatcher will ask for this information when a call for an ambulance is placed.

Equipment malfunction/failure

Is the equipment you use fit for purpose and in full working order. It is your responsibility to periodically test it, always do this at the start of your shift. If faults are discovered report and replace items.

Postal

Where do letters and parcels get delivered, what is the process for opening them.

Many years ago I worked for a large media corporation, during this period the threat level was extremely high and during a routine conversation with a member of the post room staff I was informed quite casually that a jiffy bag containing a yellow powder had been received in the post, it was addressed to the head office. I asked where is the package now and was informed shockingly that it was placed in the overnight crate for redelivery to London where the head office was based at this time. They apparently had opened it, identified it as a non de-script yellow powder, shown it to the Health and Safety come Contingency planning officer who had only secured the role because he was a former fire-fighter. A commendable job but this alone does not make a person qualified to carry out security risk assessments in a managerial capacity without further training. He looked at the item and just informed the postal officer to reseal it and ship it on. If I had not intervened on this there was a risk of contaminating both sites. Luckily the powder was harmless and was probably someone's idea of a sick joke, but as all threats must be considered as credible until proved otherwise it should have been standard operating procedure (SOP) stopping the shipment, locking down the area and informing the authorities. This highlighted what could have been at worse a catastrophic security fail for the company or at best a PR disaster.

Blackmail

Anyone can be at risk of blackmail either due to their social activities, family or business practice. By its nature, it is the use of; or threat of use, of information that a person wishes to remain secret and as such it can be very hard to mitigate against. The victim is unlikely to report it. We can reduce the risk by restricting and monitoring access to, and the use of; information and confidential material.

Violence & Threats to life

All credible threats need to be acted on, increasing security and reporting incidents to the correct authorities. Violence and disorder can come from anywhere; members of staff, the public or on-site contractors, anyone with a grudge or those that feel hard done by all pose a risk. If you work in a retail environment you may receive aggression from those you arrest or deter from shoplifting. If you work at a leisure venue it could come from those heavy in drink. You must always consider the worst happening, think about avoidance factors to minimise the risk of occurrence but also decide whether you have the adequate tools to deal with it.

Terrorism

Terrorism can come in the form of a known threat from a credible source or as a risk assessment element. However in the modern age with the state of the world as it is terrorism should always be considered a threat regardless of the type and function of your business. It is advisable to keep up to date with current events, be aware of the news and consider the global situation. It can sometimes seem easy to focus our attention on one particular group, just because they are currently grabbing headlines. The mainstream media always seems guilty of highlighting one issue at a time possibly in an attempt to not overwhelm the public. A security professional should always consider all possibilities. Just because a group appears to be dormant it does not mean we can ignore them. We should all, no matter who we are or what our job is be vigilant and alert to the dangers of terrorism and report anything suspicious. You can check the current threat level by visiting:

www.mi5.gov.uk/home/about-us/what-we-do/the-threats/terrorism/threat-levels

UK Threat level

- **LOW**   attack unlikely
- **MODERATE**   attack possible but not likely
- **SUBSTANTIAL** attack is a strong possibility
- **SEVERE**   attack is highly likely
- **CRITICAL**   attack is expected imminently

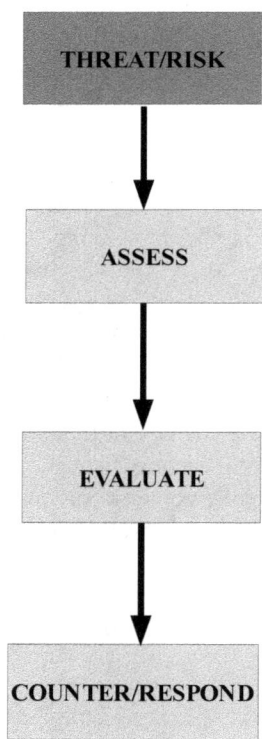

Natural Disaster/Event

If you are considering this in any great detail you either work at a static site/complex or office building employed in a primary contingency planning role or you are an extreme pessimist. As a security patrol officer you would not overly concern yourself with this unless outside environmental factors play a part. We are concentrating on the UK environment therefore unless you are providing security cover at a water dam or power plant then I think you only need to think about what natural disasters have previously affected your location of employment.

Look at all situations and possibilities and consider:

WORST CASE SCENARIO!!!!!!

By understanding the threats and risks to yourself, and your operational objectives you can highlight concerns, discuss and evaluate and decide whether a risk is acceptable or not and if necessary implement counter-measures.

It is your duty to highlight concerns. If you feel you cannot or choose not to then you are guilty of negligence. Whether your concerns are acted on or changes introduced as a result of your input is one thing. Never feel disheartened or frustrated if that is the case, know that you did what was right and what your role dictates.

Promoting a safe working environment is everyone's responsibility.

Contingency Implementation

Planning for a possible event or circumstance is a key factor to success. Good preparation and understanding of risk possibilities promotes our objective. Contingency planning is the logical next phase after the respond element.

I have purposely written this as a four phase process. Once you have identified, analysed and prioritised both Threats Phase 1, and Risks Phase 2. Then you follow the next steps of Immediate Response Phase 3 and ultimately your Phase 4 (Plan B strategy).

Threat / Risk Analysis

Is the Phase 1 threat credible (remember all are until disproved)
All threats are risks therefore Phase 2 is confirmed.

PHASE 1 THREAT

Is the Phase 2 Risk acceptable, if no continue to Phase 3

PHASE 2 RISK

Implement avoidance or deterrence counter-measures,
If unsuccessful initiate Phase 4.

PHASE 3 RESPONSE

Phase 4 activate you contingency Plan B strategy.

PHASE 4 CONTINGENCY

If we now take this into a real world situation, considering our four Phase Threat/Risk analyses imagine you are working in a retail environment consider;

Phase 2 Risk : Shoplifting

Phase 3 Response :

- CCTV and Patrol Officer deterrence
- Electronic counter-measures (tags, entry/exit alarms)
- Monitor and control of changing areas
- Staff surveillance and observation training
- Apprehension/Arrest training
- Staff ability and competence

Phase 4 Contingency :

- Non-compliant customers/offenders
- Violence
- Making off
- Possession of a weapon

The above illustrates that you need an action and response approach, if you have no response to an action then you have no use other than being a walking license holder. You have to be able to think outside the box and consider all possibilities. Communication amongst your team and operational pre-planning and assessment is key.

You also have to have contingency strategies as it creates fluidity, we cannot plan for all eventualities but we can reduce the risk of them. The point is to be confident in dealing with situations and be able to respond to them responsibly, and be aware of; and ready with other plan B contingency options should your response fail.

"He who fails to plan, plans to fail"

Winston Churchill (1874 – 1965)

CHAPTER SEVEN
Conflict Resolution

"Peace is not the absence of conflict,
but rather the ability to handle conflict by peaceful means "

Ronald Reagan

It is unfortunate but any situation which brings people together can result in conflict. This is not a pessimistic view of society it is pure logic. It is your job to mitigate against the risk and respond swiftly if it does. Resolving and reducing conflict situations in our environment not only makes things safer for others but also reduces the risk to ourselves. However many fail to understand this and take a one upmanship approach. Those that take aggression personally or as a challenge to their masculinity have no place in the security industry and are actually often only projecting their own insecurities.

Conflict can enter any situation at any time and a security professional understands this and assesses all situations prior to involvement and throughout. It happens all too often that those employed to maintain safety, often while responding to an incident, become blinkered. By failing to assess information received or ploughing into the middle of a situation and reacting poorly in order to maintain the illusion of looking tough, end up putting themselves and others at increased risk. If you ask those that work within the Close Protection framework what is the best way to deal with conflict they will tell you first and foremost that avoidance is the best way. If you can eliminate the risk altogether then the problem is solved, although continual re-assessment is needed. For those that are venue based providing policing style security your initial assessment would not need to be specifically targeted to an individual or action, and would be more general in application until an incident specific response was needed. However the same primary principle of avoidance if at all possible and continual assessment still applies.

As stated every situation should be considered and assessed for potential conflict risk. Sometimes the simplest task dealing with the calmest of people will escalate, and if dealt with correctly those which start as an incident of aggression can be calmed. No situation is typical nor are the people involved. Some of the calmest acting and well dressed people can flair up, and some that would fill you with dread on initial view turn out to be the nicest. The point is never judge a book by its cover, utilize common sense while still avoiding complacency.

Warning Signs of Aggression

Every situation, task and endeavour we undertake elicits an emotional response however emotions can often be overwhelming and difficult to control. Anger towards some actions can be justifiable but our reaction and how we deal with that anger may not be. As a security professional you need to remain calm during pressurised situations and do all you can to reduce and de-escalate aggression in others. When we become angry we become focused on irrational thought with all logic quickly vanishing. Therefore anger within ourselves is self defeating.

When dealing with others there are many warning signs and indicators towards aggression. These should be added to your situation assessment and monitored for throughout.

Consider

Aggression

Indicator

Responses

When our emotional state goes beyond our normal levels we demonstrate not only controlled but also uncontrolled actions. This stems from the principles of fight or flight and is hard wired. Some are subtle in nature where others are more obvious.

Some Aggression Indicator Responses could be;

- Standing tall/Raising their frame
- Body tension

- Restlessness
- Prolonged eye contact
- Exaggerated body movement and gestures
- Erratic movements
- Rapid breathing
- General over arousal of body system
- Raised voices
- Fear
- Threats
- Appearing withdrawn or dissociated
- Face becomes flushed
- A staggered stance
- Scanning for target acquisition (they look and assess you and your colleagues)
- Clenching fists
- Stiffening jaw, clenching teeth
- Blocking escape routes
- Verbally reporting or informing you of violent feelings

*"10% of conflicts are due to difference in opinion
90% are due to wrong tone of voice."*

We now know that running into situations blindly can be counter productive. There have been countless occasions where a security officer has ran into a possible hostile situation and instantly placed themselves in the position of going toe to toe with the loudest person involved. This is not only foolish as it does nothing to de-escalate the situation, but it can also be dangerous for all concerned. Not only does the person go on the defensive but your close proximity puts you at risk of physical assault. Doing so also affects your ability to fully observe the scene, the actions of individuals and in a worse case scenario the drawing of a weapon. It is advisable to avoid conflict, but not always possible to do so. Conflict should never be a result of your actions, being the catalyst for such events serves no-one least of all you.

In many situations being so close to another person increases hostility. It also gives you the illusion of focussed attention. If tempers are high and voices are raised your attention is often drawn to one element of the situation. This is a normal psychological reaction to someone shouting aggressively but by increasing your personal risk, by placing yourself in immediate harms way, you become unable to focus on all the elements of the encounter. Their verbal onslaught may mask not only their physical response but also the response to the situation from others around you, especially if this person came with friends.

Positioning and Personal Space

When dealing with any incident how you position yourself to others either increases or decreases risk. It is logical to consider if you are at risk of being punched standing further than arms reach reduces the immediate chance of a first strike. An aggressor would have to move in order to make contact and by doing so would alert you prior to the punch making contact. Avoiding someone's personal space also allows you to visually absorb things which may be in your periphery and get a greater visual picture of the situation.

When you think of positioning and personal space think

P.A.L.M

PALM stands for;

Position

Attitude

Look/Listen

Manoeuvre

Position

When you consider your position when dealing with an incident you must take into account your personal safety and the safety of the person you are dealing with. Invading the personal space of others is dangerous and antagonistic. Likewise if they are aggressively invading your space you avoid this by stepping back. This opens up the ground, moving you out of the danger zone and allows you to remain fully observant of the situation.

Interaction Zones

DANGER ZONE

0 – 1.0 metres
Also known as the contact zone
It is antagonistic
Only enter to make an arrest/restrain/assist

SAFETY ZONE

1.0 – 3 Metres
Facilitates communication
Allows for interaction
Good situation awareness

PUBLIC ZONE

3 Metres and over
Observational area
Non incident specific
Free movement

By following this traffic light system when it comes to interaction we are consciously aware of our position and the positions of others when dealing with incidents. Expanding on the observational principles towards keeping you safe, your position will be dictated by the actions of others during any given situation. If you are the first person on the scene of an incident or interaction, if that interaction is conversational in nature and non aggressive your initial location would logically be within the yellow safety zone. This allows you to talk to and observe those involved in a non threatening manner. If other officers attend they should at this point remain positioned in the green public zone, but at the same time keeping eyes on you and those with whom you are dealing. This is a form of non threatening positioning. They are not antagonising the situation, but they are close enough to react should the need arise or if the person initially dealing with the situation requires support or assistance. By maintaining good positioning the FPOS and any supporting officers can see not only the centre of the incident but create a reactionary perimeter.

Line Of Sight

Maintaining a good line of sight allows you to observe all that may be going on. It speeds up reaction times and increases your ability to assess situations. From the initial FPOS having a clear view of those they are interacting with, to the supporting officers being able to observe you, those you are talking to and everything going on around you, you then get the full picture and can be alerted if things change. It also allows for supporting officers to update the CCTV control room as to how the situation is progressing in order that they can further assist. For this reason it is advisable for those attending, but not directly involved in the incident, listen in to what is going on. If the situation is fast paced it is not always possible for the dealing officer to keep up to date with their radio communications and a support officer can assist with this by giving real-time radio updates.

Let us not look back in anger,
nor forward in fear,
but around in awareness

James Trigger

The position of the first additional officer/s will be determined by the type of incident and the attitude of the person being interacted with. If the situation becomes aggressive or other officers become concerned they can move closer and into the yellow safety zone. This allows for a rapid immediate response should a situation change. This situation requires continued assessment and fluid reaction. Your zone positioning will be dictated by the actions of those involved in the incident and the environment in which it takes place. These are guidelines, they are not set in stone and should be treated in line with other considerations. Positioning which makes you ineffective as a responder either by being to far away or so close you cause hostility benefits no one.

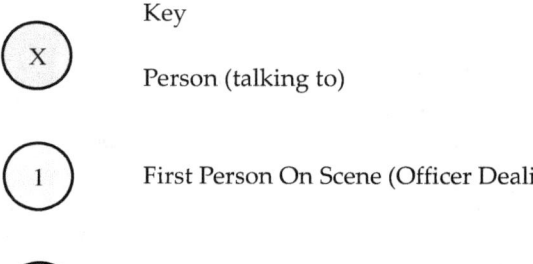

Key

X   Person (talking to)

1   First Person On Scene (Officer Dealing)

2   Additional Officer (Support)

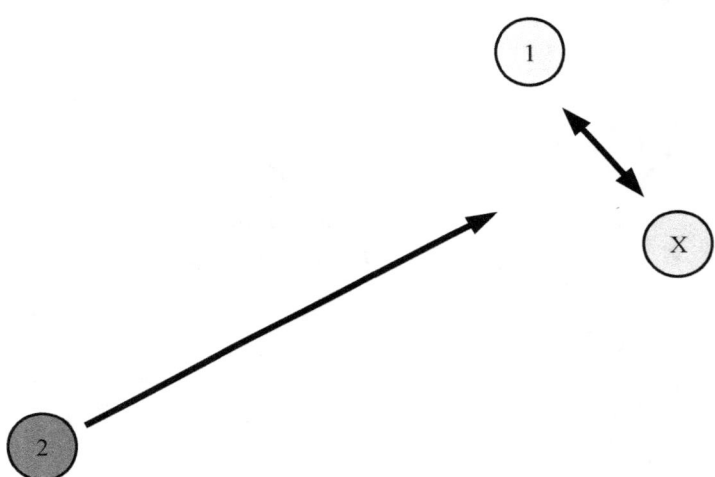

Officer 1 is positioned in the safety zone allowing for non threatening interaction. Officer 2 is positioned in the public zone, allowing them to observe, react, assist and report.

If further officers attend there is often a temptation for those officers to cluster. This is an ineffective use of operational positioning. On arrival at a scene it is acceptable for arriving officers to approach the officer in position 2 in order to be appraised of the situation but after they have been updated they should relocate to a better vantage point.

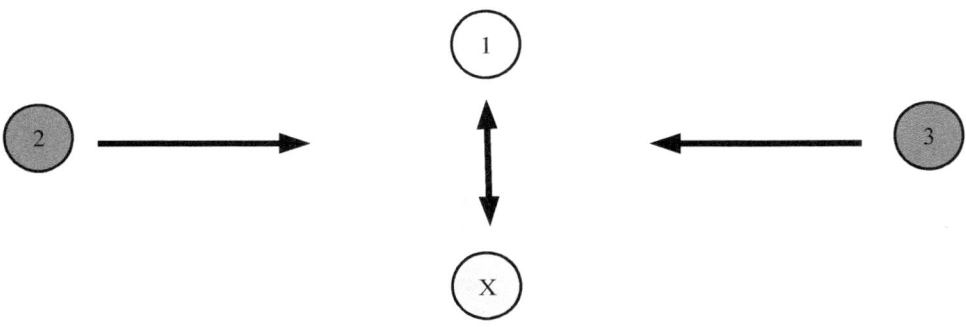

Establishing these positions increases your overall angle of observation.

This is another exercise in common sense. If the situation is relating to a member of the public which is purely seeking advice, then setting up a perimeter and implementing a heavy presence is not necessary. We are expanding on a simple principle of dealing with the public in relation to an escalating threat situation.

Attitude

How you act towards others has great bearing on how situations progress. Your attitude to not only yourself, but to members of the public and your colleagues can dictate how productive your work and indeed your life is. Having a professional attitude to your role and a respect for your profession and those you work alongside is paramount. Combine that with an understanding of all within the working environment and the ability to sympathise and empathise with those who may be in distress facilitates positive outcomes. Some situations may elicit more of an emotional connection than others. You may be able to relate to incidents personally but this is where your professionalism will be tested. It is not a case of disassociation but rather the ability to understand whilst still implementing a professional impartiality. Having a positive attitude towards your role and helping others does not always mean being so upbeat you are bordering on annoying. It is the process of offering assistance to others and promoting a professional and safe environment.

Look and Listen

Pay attention to others. Whether that is a customer or members of the public asking for advice or assistance, or a colleague or supervisor passing on information or instructions. Receiving auditory or visual information, processing and responding to it makes you a productive and reliable member of the team. If you react poorly to a situation because you failed to pay attention the fault rests on your shoulders.

Manoeuvre

We have considered incident positioning. Manoeuvring into a position to optimise effectiveness promotes a positive outcome. We have also discussed positioning in relation to personal safety and the safety of others. By establishing optimum positions it allows us to re-evaluate effectively and react whilst manoeuvring out of danger.

The SAFER Approach

You should by now be thinking how all considerations and actions are broken down into stages. From assessing risk to implementing strategies. If we work through the process regardless of whether we are dealing with an incident or just carrying out a simple task we are helping to create a conditioned response. By viewing a task as a staged process we can more easily tackle each step taking that task to a successful conclusion.

Therefore always consider the SAFER approach:

S = STEP BACK

A = ASSESS THREAT

F = FIND HELP

E = EVALUATE

R = RESPOND

Step Back

Avoid rushing into situations. Take time to stop and think. This is not to say you halt dead in your tracks and it is understandable that with some situations speed is of the essence. This is just to highlight the importance of having all the information required to understand and deal with the situation, whilst being as prepared as possible to react professionally and effectively.

Assess Threat / Situation

Identify potential threats, people, objects, places (POP) to yourself and others, scan the environment and consider the dangers involved with the situation and other possible outside factors that may affect outcome.

Find Help

Consider what assistance you may need, whether that be further officers to the scene or CCTV assistance. Do you require emergency services? Communicate your needs effectively.

Evaluate Options

Think about the options available and decide on a course of action.

Respond

Finally we implement our response, while continually reassessing and adapting if necessary.

With practice, as with all processes your reaction times will increase. When we first consider stages of evaluation as with all new experiences we tend to focus heavily on each point. But by continually thinking about and implementing life situations as stages in a process we will start to condition ourselves to respond without conscious thought. Carrying out this process regularly will compound this as an Immediate Action Response in all we do. If you can take this approach with all situations it will become second nature, and by using it to assess simple tasks means when an emergency arises the process kicks in without you even thinking about it.

Stepping back from aggression

We are now going to consider the term stepping back in a literal sense. We live in a world where we are often told never back down, stand your ground, show no sign of weakness and this is endemic especially when it comes to the security industry. However it is this attitude that separates those that just show up and collect a pay cheque from those who are the true professional. First and foremost when confronted with aggression, stepping back and removing yourself from the danger zone minimises risk and takes you out of imminent danger.

"Conflict cannot survive without your participation"

Wayne Dyer

But it also has a greater benefit, if we consider our actions as a process. By stepping back whilst verbally engaging with the aggressor we are demonstrating a non threatening demeanour but at the same time showing to those around, and sometimes more importantly to the recording CCTV operator that we are demonstrating non aggression and allowing the aggressor the opportunity to do the same. The fact we showed continuity in our actions demonstrate that we gave the aggressor opportunity to stop however should they continue to demonstrate aggressive behaviour it provides greater validation should you have to either defend yourself or physically restrain the offender. You must remember that any CCTV footage obtained is evidence of what occurred but it is video evidence and does not contain sound, therefore talking to an aggressor alone will not demonstrate to those watching the recording your intent. Visible actions on your part allow you to show you were actively trying to diffuse the situation. It will also back up your reports and your statement should you need to give one.

CHAPTER EIGHT
Immediate Action

*"The way to get started is to
quit talking and begin doing."*

Walt Disney

Immediate Action Drill (IAD) refers to your considered response for a particular incident, situation, dilemma or threat. By understanding the principles of risk a strategy can be established and an immediate action plan formulated. For example when dealing with an alleged theft you have to establish details such as who is the victim and what evidence is available to confirm or disprove the allegations. Therefore you should be considering a plan for immediate action in order to counter all the challenges presented.

If you have never considered assessing or re-evaluating your actions either prior to implementing them, or using them to assess how successful you have been in order to discover whether what you did at any given time during a incident or task could have been done differently or better. If you have never considered applying the SAFER approach then it is time to start. Whether you work in the industry already or are new to the sector, you should be thinking about events you have been involved in or those you may come across in the future, assessing the risks and comparing and considering your response.

*"Action is the foundational
key to all success."*

Pablo Picasso

It must be remembered assessment and evaluation of an incident is not a process to point fingers or establish or direct blame. It is a process to understand what went well and what went wrong in order to reduce the chance on it happening again. We learn and grow from our mistakes as well as our successes.

With the above in mind lets take a few different dilemmas, incidents and duties, and break them down. I have purposely added a non emergency situation in order to point out and remind you that this should be a process for all assessment regardless of its nature. In doing this for all things and continually repeating this action in a safe and sometimes mundane situation we condition ourselves to routinely respond in an ordered manner in both routine operations and emergency situations.

S

A ──────▶ 4 STAGE THREAT / RISK ASSESSMENT

F

E

R

Example 1

Immediate Action on – Alleged Theft

Step back – You are responding to reports of an alleged theft, at this time nothing is proven, your role is to be impartial and to establish if any offences have occurred. By not rushing in you will not react poorly.

Assess – Assess the immediate threat and risk not only to yourself but to all involved, whether that be risk of injury or risk to loss of evidence, talk to those involved, separate parties establishing who is the alleged victim and who is the alleged offender.

Find help – Utilize CCTV and colleague support if needed.

Evaluate the evidence, secure witness statements and CCTV if available.

Respond to the evidence presented. If it warrants and is practicable to do so in order to prevent an offender making off arrest and caution the alleged offender. Detain safely and lawfully request police attendance.

Example 2

Immediate Action on – Fire Alarm Activation

Stepping back may seem contradictory as time is of the essence in this situation, but it is not a literal term it is just the means of establishing the facts in a running order and knowing you must act timely but professionally. If you are responding to a request given over the radio net or as a result of an auditory alarm this time should be used to alert others.

Assess threat whilst on route by obtaining any intelligence that may be available from sources such as visible camera patrols from a CCTV source which can be relayed to you. Or technical information from a control centre. On arrival make your own visual assessment and if possible speak to others on scene to establish the cause of the fire alarm activation. If available, and there is one on scene, report information displayed on the fire panel in that location.

Find help by utilizing all available resources to establish what has occurred.

Evaluate what you discover at the scene. Check all locations, sweep the area, check voids and evaluate the fire panel. Inspect smoke heads, assess for smoke/smells in the atmosphere and obtain witness reports. Is there visible fire or indicating factors?

Response should be clear and concise, "No smoke, no fire, cause of activation is (X) panel reads (XXXXX) or Fire at location (XXXXXX) spreading, unable to tackle requesting fire appliance attendance initiating evacuation procedure all available officers to my location to assist.

As mentioned in an earlier chapter, having emergency response codes in this situation clears the net of non emergency traffic, mobilises other officers and speeds up your response.

Example 3

Immediate Action on - Customer Service Request

Step back – in this situation this is the listening phase, a person is making a request for assistance in the capacity of information.

Assess their request

Find help, if you don't know the answer then seek out those which do

Evaluate their request, and how you can professionally assist

Respond by offering and providing solutions.

Example 4

Immediate Action on – Physical Altercation (Fight)

Step back, you witness two men fighting and you may feel like running into the middle to break it up. This is a natural response but you are not down the pub with your mates, this is a professional situation. You do not know if these men have concealed weapons or if they are actually alone or if there are others just waiting to get involved.

Assess the situation, who may be involved and what is occurring.

Find help by requesting assistance and if possible getting CCTV coverage.

Evaluate the risks and the situation and decide on your options.

Respond by separating the parties, interviewing them to establish what has occurred, impartially establish the evidence and investigate and report any offences. Offer and administer first aid if required.

"Working for the benefit of others requires action,
Failing to act benefits no-one, least of all ourselves"

P.J Mac

There are no hard and fast rules, especially in life it must be remembered that all approaches are merely guidelines to point those within the sector in the right direction. It is the responsibility of the individual to adapt and implement them.

CHAPTER NINE
Tactical Dynamic Control

Every interaction with members of the public whether requiring assistance, or those situations where the intervention of security personnel is required for matters of disorder must be dealt with in a controlled manner. The level of control and style must be dynamically assessed throughout the interaction, as those we are dealing with and the reasons are often unknown. A situation which appears passive one minute could rapidly deteriorate and others which appear aggressive may be on investigation totally the opposite. Things are not always as they seem and by committing emotionally to one course of action and sticking to that action without understanding the reasoning can often cause more tension and increase the time needed to reach the required outcome.

One of the main problems when it comes to training, and especially anything which involves staff training regarding public interaction, is they often provide only operational training which they are required to by law focussing primarily on customer service assistance style training, leaving the operator to decide how he or she is going to react in difficult and demanding situations. This ambiguous approach often results in a clash between the security operative and the company or client when the employer deems actions to be contrary to their vision, it can leave the inexperienced officer confused and sometimes unable to, or unwilling to act in certain situations.

In order to operate in a Tactically Dynamic Controlled manner you must understand the two forms involved, which are Passive Control and Assertive Control. The situation as it presents itself will dictate whether a passive approach or an assertive one is required. Most situations will present themselves firstly as passive, they involve situations of required assistance, providing help or relaying information. Assertive control is needed for situations where aggression has already occurred and manifested as an indictable offence, or where you have a justifiable belief that an indictable offence is imminent. However many incidents which do require a rapid assertive response often present themselves with providing a period of passive intervention. Sometimes they may not, such as in cases where loss of life or physical assault is taking place. But by rapidly assessing your approach, you can either use or discount the passive option but by making this evaluation it adds to the justification of your actions.

Tactical Dynamic Control is implemented in two forms:

1) PASSIVE
2) ASSERTIVE

Passive Control

This is used in situations which are considered as non emergency, any role which is more assistance orientated, investigative or giving advice or reassurance. It is a situation where you are working with the co-operation of those you are interacting with whilst at the same time taking control by guiding the outcome. To do this we need to build rapport.

Rapport

CONNECT + LISTEN + RESPECT + RELATE = TRUST
(CREATING RAPPORT)

Rapport is a close harmonious relationship which promotes trust and good communication. The majority of situations dealt with on a daily basis will involve rapport. Building it not only promotes team cohesion, it is also beneficial in all situations involving others. Establishing rapport from the outset promotes confidence and trust.

Understanding Rapport

Rapport with others eases tension and de-escalates hostility. It levels the playing field and puts you on an equal footing with those you are dealing with. It allows you to empathise with others and be sympathetic to their situation and it creates an environment where your assistance and help is accepted more easily.

Building Rapport

Rapport is easier to build if you address it from the outset. If it becomes a secondary concern you may find it much harder to establish as first impressions count, and are harder to shake once an initial belief has been established. Therefore remembering our Attitude, Standards and Dress (ASD) goes a long way to creating the correct response in others. Actively listen to those you are talking to and pay attention to what they are saying, use facial expressions which sympathise and reflect the situation, be interested in them and there concerns and be empathetic. Matching tone of voice and pace of speech can often help those addressing you to feel more comfortable and more familiar. By maintaining eye contact for 60% of the time in conversation you can demonstrate you are listening and taking interest but at the same time not appear over imposing or intimidating. Actively mirroring the positioning and stance of others also helps them to feel that you understand their situation. These are subtleties to implement, you are not mimicking the other person in speech or stance as this could make the situation much worse and you are not demonstrating aggression if another is doing so, it is a means of showing you can empathise not add fuel to a fire. Implementation of an active common sense approach to the needs of the situation is definitely needed.

Listening Skills

This may seem like something that is a natural ability, without the involvement of any skill. In fact if you believe that you are confusing listening with hearing. We can all hear sounds and words, but without understanding meaning and context we are not listening. The ability to listen is a skill that all security professionals need to master whether formulating a plan of operation, speaking to an offender, victim, witness or colleague. Understanding detailed information is the best route to success.

Demonstrating Active Listening

The following is a list of ways to demonstrate you are actively listening to the person you are talking to, however this should be a natural act not something you are forcing. Nor is it something you should be concentrating on over actually listening to what's being said. If you are stood thinking and concentrating just on stance and facial expressions and trying to mirror their actions you may find yourself at the end of the conversation wondering what the hell they actually said. This list is by no means extensive nor is it acceptable for all situations.

Smile

If the situation warrants it then use small smiles, they confirm understanding and interest in what the other person is saying.

Nodding Head

When in conversation nodding your head intermittently in agreement confirms that you sympathise and understand, it promotes trust.

Eye Contact

Actively maintaining eye contact demonstrates you are paying attention, however this should not be throughout the conversation as it may appear intimidating, it is not a staring contest remember.

Posture

Your posture should not be rigid, but it should remain professional.

Distraction

It goes without saying that you should never allow yourself to be distracted, give situations your full attention but also remain alert to your surroundings. Being casually distracted in the form of not paying attention is disrespectful and rude, being professionally distracted by an event that's importance supersedes that which you are attending is justifiable. The point here is pay attention but don't be solely blinkered by it, concentrate but remain alert.

Mirroring

As stated in building rapport, mirroring is a useful tool although it must be remembered this is a subtle action and you are not out to copy positioning and stance.

Verbal Reinforcement

Verbal positive reinforcement is an action which should be used sparingly and at the right times, caution must be used when doing so as you may inadvertently emphasis a phrase or distract from the communication being received. It also assists in situations where encouragement to speak may be needed. However overuse of positive reinforcement can sometimes demonstrate insincerity. Using words of agreement, like "yes" and " I understand" and even "thank you" not only acknowledge you are listening and are absorbing what's being said, it is also polite.

Remembering

It is often difficult to remember details, this is a normal human trait but remembering specific points in relation to what's being said can be much easier to retain. So try and focus on key events of the conversion if a lot of information is being passed. However as you should be aware we ALL carry a pocket book and by taking notes the risk of missing something should be reduced.

Questioning

This is a useful tool it not only reinforces that you are paying attention but it allows you to clarify events and obtain further detail.

Clarification

Never be afraid to clarify what has been said, you may sometimes feel reluctant to do so for fear that the person will think you have not been listening. Failing to clarify or highlight points of confusion can mean that you are operating on mis-information which can not only increase your work load, as you may end up wasting time doing the wrong thing. If you are involved in investigating a crime or dealing with disorder failing to prepare and clarify details may result in very shaky legal grounding for your actions.

Reflection and Review (Assessment)

Reflection of the information can be done by paraphrasing what has been said. It shows an understanding but promotes thought of what has been communicated. Allowing for your own internal assessment of the details and facts and views to take place.

Tactical Communication

To do this you need to be knowledgeable about what you are doing and the advice and support you give. You have to have confidence in your skills and promote that confidence in others by projecting yourself well. Your vocal responses must be distinct and clear. Avoid using slang words and maintain eye contact with those you are addressing. Using hand signals and gestures to direct others, conveying your wishes to warn of hazard and promote avoidance. Your voice and actions must be fluid in nature whether passing instruction or seeking support and assistance, being understood and keeping people up to date with what you need them to do or how you are helping them reassures and promotes compliance.

Social Compliance

Contrary to what you may feel and sometimes think at work most people are socially compliant and will often happily follow instruction provided it is given in a professional manner. We all do this automatically, from following street signs and signs on doors, to arrows on a walkway. These things are all put in place to promote compliance and failing the introduction of an issue that creates disruption, they work perfectly. This occurs because people are often reluctant to appear out of the ordinary, and avoid standing out and drawing attention.

The subtle promotion of this works well as it succeeds to facilitate the operators wish to control the actions of others whilst at the same time the public's wish to comply and maintain anonymity. However when situations change abruptly it will often require the involvement of security personnel. The willingness of an individual to comply when they are in a confused situation can sometimes be suspended due to their ignorance of an issue and it is often purely down to the tact of those attempting to intervene that either creates success or failure. For example if a persons direction of travel is hindered due to an incident or safety issue, the placement of a security officer now being a barrier to a persons expectations, confusion and hostility may result. Initially their lack of compliance may be purely down to the simple fact of limited information and all that is needed is a little customer service professionalism to guide and advise.

Successful promotion of compliance can be achieved through something as simple as providing a uniformed presence. People are programmed to conform to authority and a figure in a uniform reinforces this, providing they are dressed correctly in a uniform which is fitted. If you combine this professional look and presence with a confident and well informed attitude, the guidance of the officer and instruction will be more easily accepted and acted on. If an officer has a poor or negative attitude and this is combined with poor drills and training it then becomes self defeating. It would be logical on reading this to automatically be drawn to think of a time when this compliance did not occur. You may have done all the above and it did not work. We are not at this point referring to isolated incidents of aggression or non compliance from an individual. We are talking about the public as a whole and the willingness to follow clear and conformist instruction not the actions of a minority group or individual.

Assertive Control

Assertive control is the means of taking absolute control of a person or situation in order to preserve life and protect against injury. It is a sad fact that in the modern age employers promote all kinds of customer service training emphasising being polite, helpful and providing service and information to the customer. These are all good and necessary qualities but they overlook training which brings out confidence and assertiveness as they may not feel it fits with the companies image.

The question should be asked especially in the security environment what do you want your security to be, an illusion of service or an active promoter of safety?

Whether you work in a warehouse or a hotel or even a shopping centre good customer service is needed and your approach to it will be dictated by your environment, but surely the first primary principle for those operating in the security sector should be the preservation of life and reducing the risk of injury. Security employment within the hospitality sector is increasingly becoming an avenue for those that possess customer relations skills over security ones. In reality the two should go hand in hand. If all you can ever offer is a smile and information without understanding and being able to pro-actively minimise risk whilst at the same time responding to threat, please do not call yourself security as you may be on paper employed to provide that service but you are not offering it. This is often not the fault of the individual rather of the employer wishing to be seen to provide one service when in fact they are offering something completely different, and far less effective.

SECURITY + CUSTOMER SERVICE = **SUCCESS**

CUSTOMER SERVICE – SECURITY = **FAIL**

When it comes to dealing with incidents we should be assessing them continually throughout. Some may start passive and end requiring the application of Assertive Control, never be afraid to be assertive providing your actions are lawful and justified. Understanding and confidently implementing Assertive Control of a situation is part of your Immediate Action. As said in the introduction to this chapter in order to dynamically operate in the assertive phase you should, if practicable to do so, have passed through or assessed it as not possible due to the nature of the event the passive phase. The justification for not doing so will be dictated by the incident itself. If you are responding to intelligence of a fight and on arrival find two males arguing you would attempt to pacify the situation, if however blows were being exchanged then you would need to assert control by possibly restraining the offenders.

Situations

Situations in which assertive control may be needed.

For Example

- Preservation of life
- Resisting lawful arrest
- Violent disorder

- Assault
- Fire or Hazardous material
- Building unsafe
- Terrorism

Verbal Compliance

Assertive verbal compliance can be used in any of the above situations and can be justified, for instance in the event of a known fire situation you may request polite passive compliance, unfortunately you are being ignored and the person continues their course of action, increasing risk not only to themselves but also to others. You can by demonstrating a clear passive attempt to promote compliance justify adapting to a more assertive approach.

In order to inform and control the public in high risk situations, raising your voice and giving clear instructions not only allows your colleagues to know what you are doing it gives your instructions as orders and not as a request. This is especially useful if a person is committing an offence or action which endangers either their life or the lives of others, and claim later that they did not hear the instruction.

Adding a little clarity!

There is a right time and wrong time to use verbal compliance and it should be obvious, barking orders because you are angry that a person has parked a car in a location which offends you or because they missed the bin with a piece of litter is not what we would call justifiable. Shouting instructions to a violent offender, or to a member of the public entering an area of a chemical spill or fire where there is a risk of injury or loss of life is.

Signals and Gestures

When operating in high tension situations you may want to give inappropriate hand signals and gestures but being a professional used to working under pressure I'm sure you do not. We are actually referring to clear instructional hand signals, being able to convey instruction both visually and verbally reinforces those instructions, imagine a police officer controlling traffic or ground crew taxiing an aircraft on the airport apron. They are conveying non verbal instruction which can be clearly understood with just their hands and arms.

Physical Compliance

Any person operating in the security industry should be trained in physical intervention, and have a good understanding of positional asphyxiation. This training provides operational guidelines but responsibility for your actions and justification lies with the individual. You cannot be afraid to physically restrain or redirect a person if you can lawfully justify it.

Tactical Compliance

Tactical compliance is the utilization of all the above compliance methods. Initiating verbal, signal and physical compliance techniques in order to promote a desired outcome. That being to preserve life, prevent injury, deter and prevent crime and disorder.

Uses

- To disorientate and control aggressive offenders
- To promote compliance in an emergency
- To warn others

CCTV & Tactical Compliance

CCTV is used to monitor the safety of all who are within that environment. The material gathered should be held in line with the Data Protection Act 1998 and also for evidential purposes. Therefore in situations of aggression, hostility or violence your actions may be called into question and you may have to justify why you carried out one particular course. By using Tactical Compliance your clear verbal instruction to an individual or suspected offender would be overheard and confirmed by any witness's and your signals and gestures will be recorded by the CCTV cameras. These two forms of evidence then promote the justification aspect of the physical compliance element.

Example

A person is clenching their fists and shouting as they aggressively approach you in a hostile manner:

You take assertive control implementing tactical compliance

Verbal (loud and Clear)

GET BACK !!!   GET BACK!!!   GET BACK!!!

Signal / Gesture

RAISE ARMS TOWARDS THE AGRESSOR / PALMS FLAT TOWARDS THEM

In doing so you are conveying a message which will be clearly understood. Your actions can be confirmed by others and you can demonstrate your intentions on CCTV.

Complaints

Proactive officers may receive conduct complaints, either in the form of verbal threats or complaints to colleagues, written or even ones which result in police or company investigation. This can be rather daunting or disheartening especially when in your mind all you have done is act in good faith by trying to help. You cannot do your job and keep everybody happy, after all if you detain and arrest a person on suspicion of an offence they will probably not be to happy about it. It is also possible that in some situations witness's to your actions may make complaints. This occurs as they are seeing your actions from their own separated view point and are not in full possession of the facts. Your conduct may be called into question and this is why understanding the law, being of good character and being able to justify your actions is of paramount importance. Never allow the fear of complaint or repercussions to detract you from your duties. It is very easy for those with weak character or those fearful of an outcome to use this consideration to justify in their own mind not taking action or responding to a request for assistance. However in doing so you may be putting others in danger, and the situation you avoid today could repeat involving you tomorrow. How would you feel if others acted the same way, leaving you to deal with a dangerous situation on your own.

CHAPTER TEN
Incident Investigation

*"No person can hope to
discover truth without investigation."*

George Richards

In order to establish events and therefore act accordingly you must start by investigating the incident. In some cases this may seem easy, the evidence and reports of what has occurred are visually obvious. Unfortunately in many cases an incident or dilemma will require more in depth analysis. Remember before you can act in any situation you need to assess the scene and circumstances, understand it and then decide on a course of action. This requires a calm level headed approach. Analysing the data, evidence and witness accounts obtained gives the fullest picture possible of what has occurred. All incidents should be addressed from a professional impartial position, you are dealing in facts and you follow the evidence, personal opinion and sympathies should in no way direct your actions. It is much easier to gather evidence while it is fresh, for the security officer this should be a matter of course as you will be responding in real time. Depending on the nature of the incident you are investigating tensions may be high amongst aggrieved parties, it can take time to establish what has actually taken place. In situations such as this it is the duty of the officer to calm and control the situation in order to progress and facilitate a smooth investigation.

One of the first things you must establish if you are responding to a criminal incident is who if anyone is the aggrieved party, put in simple terms is there an alleged victim. We use the term alleged because the nature of our legal system is based on the presumption of innocence until proven guilty. For the average security officer the type of incidents that you may come across could be ones of disorderly conduct, theft or criminal damage. Although if you work at a busy location you would probably consider these things as a mere 1/10 of the incidents you deal with. But these have been highlighted due to their repetitive nature, they reflect the two types of aggrieved party. All demonstrate either crimes against a person or crimes against property. For example one person punches another, the incident is caught on camera and the other person does not react or strike back. We have the evidence to indicate the alleged aggrieved party, we can identify an assault has occurred and identify that one offence, but further investigation will need to be undertaken immediately to establish the reasoning and whether other offences have been committed.

In the case of damage to property or theft from your employer the aggrieved party is the company, and the company not the individual prosecutes for the offence. You as an agent of your employer facilitates the smooth investigation and collation of the data and evidence, by acting to prevent and apprehend the alleged perpetrator from making off or by securing evidence of the offence for later arrest by the police.

Scene Snoopers

It is wise to assess and evaluate how you deal with an incident scene, both by way of planning your actions prior to deployment and also debriefing after an event. Not only to improve your own professionalism, but all incidents attract public attention and in this modern age where every man and his dog pulls out their phones to record what's going on any mistakes, breaches of the law and or stupidity often makes its way onto social media, or worse is then used as evidence against you. This does not mean you should detract yourself from the operation at hand to start interacting with those filming it. This is just to remind you that your professionalism or lack of; is on show for the world to see. Remember in a public place people have the legal right to film you and you cannot stop them. In a private venue permission must be sought but it is a civil issue which should only be dealt with retrospectively, however this is often infeasible and impractical to do. Regardless of this any person who would stop dealing with an incident to waste their time arguing with a person on the rights and wrongs of them filming needs to reassess their priorities.

Scene or Situation Investigation

This again is a common sense issue, and your actions should reflect the nature of the incident you are dealing with. It is logical to assume that an incident involving aggression or threats to life or even the loss of life would be treated and controlled in a greater fashion than a incident that may be less aggressive or violent in nature, such as structural damage to premises on a small scale. It is down to your assessment of the needs at the scene to apply the correct response. When we consider the process of investigation we are primarily looking at an incident or crime scene in relation to our immediate action in order to facilitate a smooth investigation, whether the incident is reportable to the police or not.

Approach to Action

You should by now be aware of the importance of assessing all situations in which you have dealings, not only for your own safety, and the safety of others but to increase your knowledge regarding the incident. On approaching the scene of an incident or crime you should:

1) Assess for dangers (to yourself and others)

2) Fully scan the scene and periphery

3) Obtain any intelligence that assists (CCTV Control)

4) Obtain witness accounts

5) Evaluate scene

6) Preserve Scene if required

7) Formulate and implement response

The Investigation process

Reactive Instigation

When it comes to the majority of incidents dealt with by a security officer they will be instigated as reactionary intervention, either you will react to things you have personally witnessed or under instruction from a CCTV control centre or even by means of reports received by a colleague or member of the public.

Proactive Instigation

In some cases you may be tasked to pro actively investigate an incident. This is a form of intelligence led investigation. Often used to monitor for crime repetition, putting in place officers to target particular groups or locations or a spate of a particular offences.
This is more commonly in use by police and other government agencies as it can be costly

and time consuming albeit highly effective in targeting offenders. It is a very useful approach for locations such as shopping malls and airports, anywhere with a high level of public foot traffic over a large area. However for many locations due to limited funds and manpower this may not be a feasible option.

Initial Investigation

Most incidents that you will be tasked to attend will not be serious in nature and as a result the first officer in attendance may be the only resource required to investigate and conclude the incident. It is important that the first person on scene acts quickly not only to ascertain the situation but also secure any evidence which could be lost, misplaced, stolen or damaged as time passes. You must take as much detail as possible and see the incident through to either its conclusion or until it is successfully passed to a specialist resource such as the police or other qualified body, recording all material, witness testimony and details in order to allow correct reports to be filed in accordance with both your personal and company policies. This is why we all carry pocket books!

Pocket Book

You can use your pocket book to record:

- Details of the event
- Names and addresses of persons involved, if given
- Short statements by witness,s (Signed and printed by them)
- Sketch diagrams of scene
- Your actions exactly and the actions of others
- Any suspect details, if given
- Any relevant comments by suspects or individuals in relation to events

The first officer on scene may have to deal with:

- Preventing further or continued criminality
- preventing further injury
- Public disorder
- Violent situations
- Providing First Aid
- Orchestrating additional response needs
- Prioritising aspects to be dealt with

- reassuring victims and witness's
- Calling for assistance

This may seem like a heavy burden and it is, but it reminds us that we need to follow processes in order to act fast. Whilst at the same time professionally establish the events and assist those involved. Until we have the incident under our control it is impossible to safely move forward with our investigation. The fresher the information the faster it can be investigated. Always remember the first person on scene is the one who leads the investigation. It is their job to direct others as they arrive and update them as to how things will and should progress. This is not to say that the views of others should be discounted it should be led but not blindly, if another officer has intelligence relating to what has happened it should be absorbed into your plan moving forward.

Incident Investigation Priorities

- Preserve life
- preserve scene
- Identify victims and suspects (Witness accounts)
- Identify other sources of evidence (Material – CCTV – Property Damage)
- Preserve evidential material
- Communication updates to CCTV and other officers

Scene Identification

On arrival at a crime scene the initial investigating officer should identify and establish the following:

- The victim
- The witness's
- The suspect
- What has occurred (Accounts & Continuity of evidence)
- Access, Egress and control of the situation and scene

Crime Scene Preservation

It is essential that the first officers in attendance at a crime scene immediately and thoroughly assess the needs of the incident and take control of the scene. Doing so preserves the integrity and continuity of the investigation as well as any evidence, reducing the risk of scene contamination.

It is often a rather popular action on hearing of an incident to want to attend and it is right that enough officers do so in order to assist and control an incident. This should be done with consideration of the needs of the situation and the risk of losing control of the incident, and possible destruction of evidence. Therefore a controlling perimeter should be set up and manned by later arriving officers to avoid not only those officers from further antagonising a situation but to reduce further incursion on the scene by those that have no need to be there.

Photographic Evidence

They say a picture speaks a thousand words, therefore evidence in photographic form is always beneficial. Verbal or written accounts can often be interpreted slightly differently, whereas a correctly taken picture supplied alongside other evidence helps to cement confirmation. For this section we are not referring to scenes that would be considered crimes. Incidents of that nature are rightly only to be photographed by professional police forensic (SOCO) Scene Of Crime Officers also now known as (CSI) Crime Scene Investigators. We are also not discussing it in relation to an immediate action incident. We are referring to actions which often fall under health and safety. Obtaining photographic evidence of damage to building fabric or machinery, either as part of a routine inspection or after an accident or incident involving risk or injury, and especially if medical intervention / first aid is administered. Photographs are often a requirement for insurance and investigative purposes and are to be submitted alongside the relevant documentation and available CCTV footage. A security officer may be tasked as part of the investigation to obtain a photographic account.

Any photograph taken should only contain within the frame footage that which is in relation to what needs to be conveyed. If the incident was in multiple locations then each location must be photographed and each evidential picture numbered and logged. If it is in relation to a vehicle collision or slip/trip/fall incident your investigations should already have identified direction of travel and this should be logged and approach photographs taken. When it comes to taking photographs of an incident involving building fabric/ furniture or a car then we can establish the depth and distance from the photograph, as we can all imagine the rough size of a vehicle or observe the height of a window or staircase. However this is not as easy in relation to a slip/trip/fall. When taking a picture of a raised paving stone or a pool of liquid on the floor greater accuracy may be needed in order to understand its dimensions, possessing a ruler and laying it in shot would help. Unfortunately it is unlikely you would be in possession of one, you should however in your pocket have a pen. A pen is a constant, meaning everyone can easily identify and understand its size, and by doing so can estimate the actual size of the object or substance in the photograph.

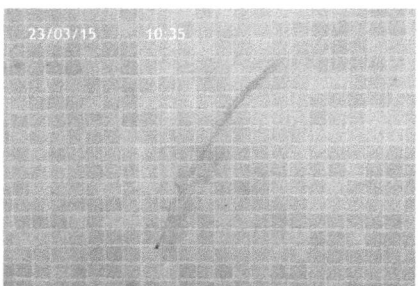

figure 1

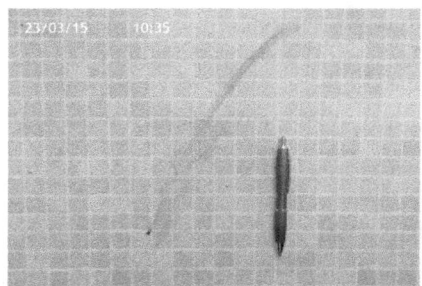

figure 2

Figure 1 identifies a mark or substance on the ground. However it is not until we review figure 2 that an estimated length of that substance can be established. As long as the item used does in no way interfere with the evidence (change or adapt it). Any item of constant shape and size may be utilised, in this case we used a pen it would be just as relevant to use your radio.

Photographic evidence must be;

- Relevant to requirements.
- Identifiable and understood.
- Numbered, logged & recorded.
- All photos must display time and date stamp.

Investigative Witness Accounts

When we consider witness accounts we are not just referring to the statements offered to us by by-standers. We are referring to the statements received by all involved during the incident. This includes the alleged victim, the alleged suspect, all who saw the event and all who are involved in your enquiries, this includes YOU!! You arrived at the scene more than likely after the event but in order to show continuity of the investigation you must not only record what others say and do but also your actions. Remember record all details of the incident, all relevant details offered by all parties. If a witness is willing ask them to confirm the details by signing and printing their name under any statement or account recorded in your pocket book. But remember again all details which are offered are voluntary, no person can be compelled to answer any request you make. However, especially when asking for details from an alleged suspect / victim, if they refuse to give an account of what occurred it is wise to record the question you asked and state their refusal to answer in your pocket book. In referring to the verbal statements offered, we are discussing the account of the incident at the scene in order to establish what has happened in order to react and record details of those involved which can then be passed to the police. We are not referring to formal witness statement accounts which are to be submitted as evidence. These are collected and dealt with by the police themselves. Incidents can and often do move quickly and it is not always practicable to obtain lots of details from lots of witness's. In such cases it may be more prudent just to obtain contact details for each and if it is warranted these can be passed to the police for them to make further enquiries. Again no one can be compelled to give you details, it is purely from a persons willingness to do so.

Initial Investigation Conclusion

In order to conclude your phase of control of an incident you must;

- Confirm that the immediate needs of the victim and witness's have been met
- Scene is safe and if required secure
- testimony from those involved has been taken and recorded
- Emergency services have been alerted if required and are in attendance
- All intelligence has been gathered, recorded and submitted

Witness Statements MG11

All that has been previously said has been in reference to obtaining and recording information in a pocket book. We are now going to look at the use of an official police witness statement form. Let me remind you we are not the police, even if reading this book may seem to show some similarities. The only similarity being that we are compelled to follow the law. It is not a security professionals role to compel people to fill out an MG11 document nor do we have any power to request them to do so. It is advisable however that as agents who often come into contact with incidents, which involve legal proceedings and police investigation, have the ability as a witness to events know how to fill out a witness statement form for ourselves. This is not a compulsory element, any police officer if required will take and record your verbal statement on a MG11 for you to confirm read and sign.

There is nothing wrong with choosing this option however there are bonuses for knowing how to write your own. The first being the statement is written whilst still fresh in your mind, remember you may refer to your pocket book whichever option you choose but the main reason a professional security operator would write their own statement is because it not only speeds up the police investigation but it also promotes your operational effectiveness. If a location requires security, they do so for a reason. If you are no longer available to carry out patrols because you and other members of your team are tied up with the police then your effectiveness suffers. The police are there to do a job but you are also there to do yours. It is a sad state of affairs that many business's especially retail outlets fail to prosecute offenders because the prosecution process can result in many staff members being called away from their duties to be interviewed by the investigating police officer. If you and the rest of the security team possess blank copies of the local relevant forces MG11s then you can rotate who stands down in order to write their statement thus reducing operational impact. The ability to carry this out and reduce the impact on your employer not only benefits them it also benefits you, companies and again I'm referring more to retail establishments which become slack in their willingness to prosecute become well known among the offender community and attacks will increase as they are seen as soft targets. This makes your role in such an establishment rather obsolete whilst at the same time increasing your staff risk of physical assault from the increased numbers of possible offenders being attracted to the store.

MG11 Confidence

All things take experience and practice to master. You can not become used to a task if you rarely take the opportunity to be involved in it. Avoidance of something that should be part of your job is unprofessional. If you do not possess the experience then some trepidation towards statement writing is understandable. You can reduce this by setting some time aside to practice. Think about an incident you have dealt with or if you are new to the industry consider any event. Take a period out of your day and practice putting that information down in statement form.

Consider all detail of fact from that period and write it with flow and continuity of the event and time period. Then read and review it, consider anything you may have missed or omitted in error. Does it follow the events in a time line and is it easy to understand as if it was being read by a third party. In doing so valuable practice and confidence can be gained at a calm pace and in a relaxed environment. If you want to add to this training practice you could make notes on your day while you are out and about. List them again as a time line, then when you get home transfer those notes into a formatted statement. This tests your writing and note taking skills placing the experience as close to reality as possible. Operationally you must be able and adept at taking quick and fast notes in short form, whilst obtaining all the necessary detail required. Doing so will highlight any areas you need to work on and detail missed whilst still in a controlled environment. Increasing your practice and confidence in this task will translate into speeding up your response in real world situations.

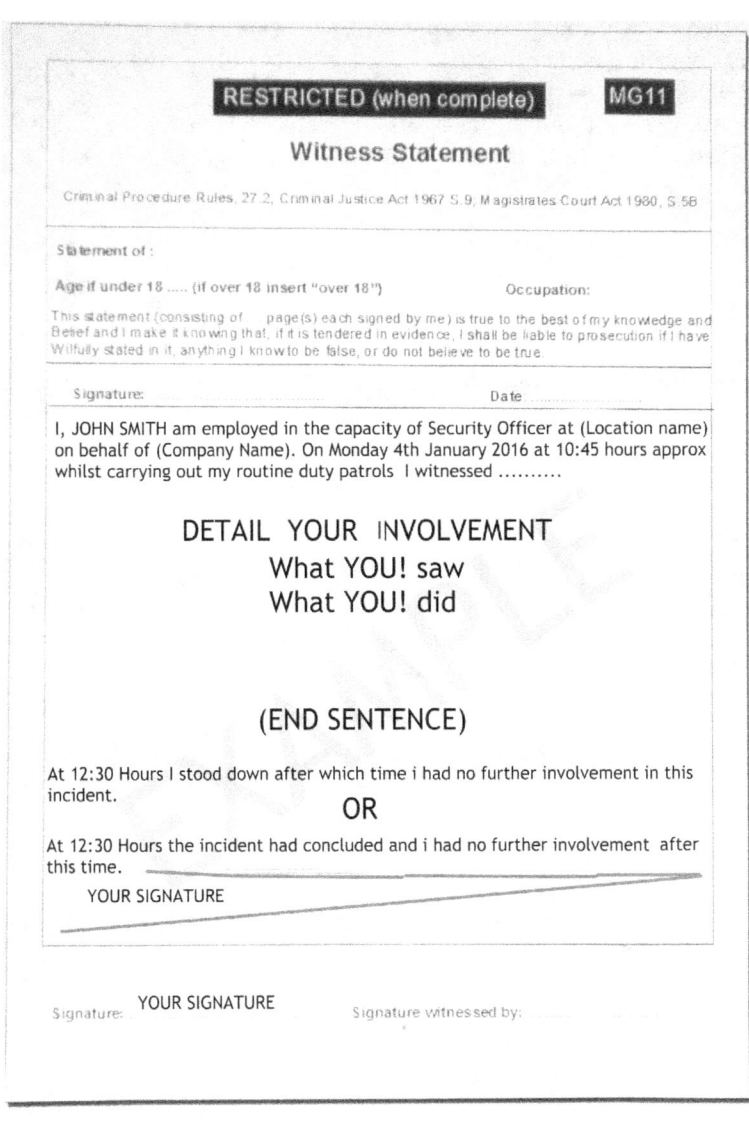

When compiling YOUR! Statement YOU MUST;

- Use only black ink
- Write normally but clearly
- Only write the facts
- Write individual names in bold
- Draw single line through blank spaces
- Sign to confirm statement
- initial all changes
- Draw a single line through any errors and initial the margin if this is the case
- treat the document in compliance with the Data Protection Act 1998

Don't

- Speculate as to events
- Add personal opinion
- Add hearsay or any views or opinions of others which bare no relation to events
- Scribble out errors

A MG11 Witness statement is a legal document and should be treated with respect, remember we are only referring to your statement of your actions. Not only for legal reasons but also for reasons of data protection you should not and must not involve yourself in filing, storing or coercing others to compile a MG11 document.

Preservation of Life / Medical Investigations

Whether you are at a crime scene or any other kind of incident, your first priority is the preservation of life. Safety to oneself as a first responder and the safety of others takes president over all other actions and you facilitate this by on arrival at the scene assessing for danger. Has that danger passed or is it still a threat? If it has passed then we can move on to the next phase, if not then we must address that danger first. All security officers should possess some formal and practical first aid training if they want to be productive in this profession.

When we refer to investigating a medical incident we are doing so in an immediate action role and not as a retrospective investigation. An incident has occurred and we are on scene to deal with it straight away. As with all investigations establishing what has happened may be obvious if there has been an accident or assault, this is known as your primary medical assessment, this covers all the visible aspects of the incident, injuries to; and affect on the casualties. While dealing with the initial obvious situation you must consider also any secondary factors such as medical conditions which may either have caused the emergency or could affect your response or treatment. In any emergency medical situation being able to quickly act and relay accurate information to the ambulance service could be life saving.

"Tomorrows victory comes from today's training"

P.J Mac

Emergency Situation and Scene

When dealing with any emergency situation always consider

- Dangers to yourself and others
- Preserving Life
- Preserving or re-establishing a safe environment - controlling the scene
- Setting up a safety perimeter and controlling access
- Communication with team, CCTV and outside agencies
- Continuity risks to the success of the operation (Evidence & Life)

CHAPTER ELEVEN
Traffic Management

There is a growing need for traffic management in the private sector. The expansion of commercial, industrial and retail sites means more and more contain privately owned road networks. In some cases due to the nature of the site and the sheer expanse it can often be hard to know where the private site ends and the public highway begins especially as new roads are built to compliment the surrounding network system. Whether you work at a large complex or are providing event security where vehicles are encouraged to come on site, you must be able to mange this flow safely. In this chapter we are referring to traffic management in regard to vehicle access on privately owned land. You do not have any right to hinder the flow or interfere with traffic on the public highway. The public highway is the responsibility of the local authority, the highways agency and the police. Putting aside the legalities of interfering on the public highway your major concern should be one of insurance. However this should not preclude you from dealing with traffic at the scene of an emergency regardless of its location, should you feel confident to do so. Remember, that which is necessary is legal and the preservation of life supersedes all things providing you can justify your actions.

Vehicle access, egress and movement while on site not only promotes the objectives of your employer, it can reduce tension and promote customer service. We can all think of more than one occasion when we have been stuck in traffic and it is not a pleasant experience. Now combine that with being either in a field trying to exit from a gig or at a retail centre just trying to leave the car park, your vehicle seemingly getting nowhere. As you look out of your car window you see a plethora of bright yellow jackets. Those employed by the venue just standing around. This can and often results in increased anger and hostility. It is not their fault there is congestion, that may well be due to the sheer volume of traffic on site or it could be due to factors off site on the local road network. But tensions are exacerbated by the lack of perceived action or customer service on the part of the security or parking staff. By doing all you can to avoid on-site congestion whilst adopting a good customer service approach and relaying information, you can promote a positive experience. We cannot always prevent events occurring but by doing all we can to rectify them when they do we can go along way to bringing about a satisfactory outcome.

The 3 main points to consider in relation to on site traffic :

1) **A = ACCESS**

2) **P = PARKING (on site movement)**

3) **E = EXIT**

Putting it in simple terms, get them in, get them parked (safely) and get them out again all in as professional a manner as possible. Many companies, especially those working at events have no problems managing points 1 and 2 but fall down on considering point 3. Not because they have managed the first two well but because arrival at the venue is often intermittent and fluid over a long period and is able to self manage the situation with little interference, providing adequate planning has been implemented on the lead up to the event starting. When it comes to step 3 often the organisers and the traffic security detail either overlook it or avoid this consideration completely, due to the conclusion of the event and possible lack of interest in their customers. However poor and delayed exiting increases risk and upsets customers. And upset and angered customers create hostility and promotes a poor reputation. Therefore a good fluid response to promote safe exit and continued movement, reducing congestion during this period is a function which should not be ignored especially if this event is ongoing or an annual occurrence.

Factors Affecting Traffic

- Site layout and space
- Traffic volume
- Weather
- Road traffic collision
- Road works
- Vehicle breakdown
- Customer service
- Signage / Assistance

Assessment

Prior to any change of circumstance feasibility should always be assessed and consideration for contingency planning approaches should be considered.

Reporting

Reports prior to any change should always be submitted in order to minimise operational impact. This should be done throughout as changes occur. Keeping your team up to date regarding events, obstructions, and changes to traffic flow/volume should be reported immediately. This includes defects to highway affecting both vehicle and pedestrian access and any traffic sign discrepancies.

Traffic Diversions

Diversions which impact on the public highway should be implemented in conjunction with the backing of the local authority and policed by that authority. However diversions on a private site should be implemented in order to promote safety and traffic flow and as a means of good customer service.

Road Obstructions

Obstructions can come in the form of other vehicles or as a result of a natural event, from flooding or fallen trees. Anything which impedes the flow of traffic and creates a hazard to vehicles and pedestrians should be reported, marked as a hazard and traffic re-directed away.

Highway Markings

Many commercial and retail sites have signs and road markings in accordance with road traffic regulations. It is the responsibility of the company and its agents to maintain these items and keep them in good working order. It is your job to report any defects as soon as they are noticed.

Temporary Signs

Temporary signs should be used to direct traffic where applicable. They should be constructed to regulation standards and placed in clearly visible locations. They should give clear and meaningful instruction to road users and early warning of hazard. Any temporary signs need to be placed and secured against tampering, and to reduce it being affected by wind and other elements. Failure to do so may increase risk to the public and eliminate its usefulness.

Vehicle Spacing

When it comes to parking vehicles on land which has no definable layout, for instance as a result of temporary change of use on a field or brown site. In using a field or wasteland to park visitors major pre-planning must be carried out in regard to management of the site. Rapid and immediate control must be implemented, as any failure to control how the vehicles line up will have a knock on effect. When it comes to lining up vehicles on unmarked land, defining layout by dimensions can often be difficult to do especially if time is a factor. Standing there with a tape measure would be time consuming and not practical, it would also not win you many friends.

Parking Principles

- Know your start point for each lane
- Understand Entrance/Exit/Approach positioning
- Keep line of parking vehicles straight
- Park vehicles forward facing (one/same direction)
- Designated areas set for similar sized vehicles (Coaches etc.)
- Allow for turning space and exit
- P ark vehicles door width apart (access)

Example

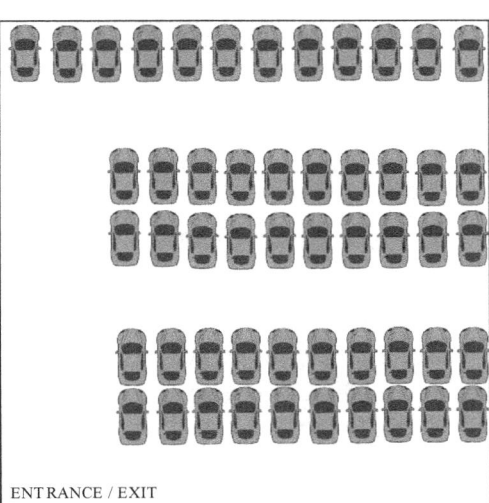

The above example allows for vehicles to be parked whilst still maintaining an area for movement and traffic flow by providing space to accommodate the influx whilst allowing for free flowing exit.

Parking Control

All mass parking must be done in a controlled manner. This can be achieved by initially starting at the furthest point and working backwards towards the entrance. In order to maintain a fluid approach to this it is advisable that an officer controls the line using hand signals to the approaching vehicles. This officer needs to be the one in control of the site. The officer in this position passes radio instructions to other officers at the influx gate to either speed up or slow access traffic. The officer in control has to send clear instruction and those assisting have to act on this instruction quickly as to avoid the control of this operation falling apart.

Communication

If communication is slow or poor it will hamper what you are trying to achieve. Give regular updates over the radio net to colleagues, team leaders and CCTV control where available. Keep line of sight to other officers on the ground and drivers entering the parking location and use clear understandable hand signals as confusion creates delays. Remember those arriving are doing so for a reason and will be happy to follow your instructions providing they are understood.

Routes in and out

All access routes need to be maintained and kept clear. This can be achieved by regular patrols and customer service. Any slight delays or stoppages can have a detrimental affect. This not only includes on and around the site but also the perimeter and access points.

Monitor

It is a good housekeeping policy not only for safety reasons but also to promote a secure environment to not only routinely monitor traffic flow but also vehicles at rest. This does not increase your liability and you are not accepting responsibility for the vehicles but routine patrols do serve to reduce the risk of theft and damage while allowing you to monitor those arriving on site and assessing any possible threat.

Traffic Officers

All those working on traffic duty must be seen. You have to remember you are dealing with active traffic. Moving vehicles are a hazard and therefore for health and safety reasons as well as promoting a visible presence you must wear high visibility clothing. Your primary piece of kit will be a High Visibility jacket. This item should be in either reflective orange or yellow. You may see some who wear black jackets with reflective strips, this style of jacket does not offer as good a reflective surface area and as such fails to do the job properly. It would be like choosing a candle over a torch to light your way in the dark. If the correct kit is available then use it. However whether you are in yellow or orange, whether in a full padded jacket or thin jacket designed to wear over your coat the garment should cover all your upper body, this includes full arm coverage.

The sleeveless style vest may be fine for pedestrian areas but it is not acceptable when dealing with vehicles in motion. You need to be noticed and the greater the reflective area the greater the chance you will be. Having full length arm coverage of reflection also means that cars will see and be able to respond to given signals.

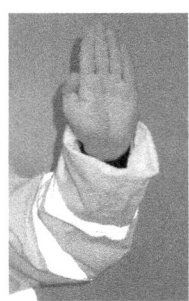

A traffic officer needs to be a team positive, action responsive person. One who can react to changing circumstance and capable of rapid assessment. To work in traffic you have to have excellent communication skills both on the radio and verbally as well as a confident instructive manner.

Road Traffic Incidents

When dealing with large volumes of traffic the risk of incident increases dramatically. In any incident our first priority is safety, to ourselves and for those involved. An incident can be in the form of a risk or an accident. For example adverse weather on the carriageway or car park such as winter ice, no accident has occurred but we must treat the incident in order to avoid the risk of an accident. The accident element is the result of the condition therefore all accidents are incidents but not all incidents are accidents.

Definitions

Incident

An instance of something happening, or that which is liable to happen because of ..... or resulting from......., an event or occurrence.

Accident

An unfortunate incident that happens unexpectedly or unintentionally, typically resulting in damage or injury.

In order to assess a road traffic incident or accident safely follow:

Dynamic Risk Assessment

Location

Consider location in relation to other road users including foot traffic, visibility of the danger and hinders to traffic flow. Promote the reduction or elimination of further risk. Set perimeter and keep area sterile.

Identify Hazards

Whether accident or incident identify what object or obstructions are involved and other hazards which may affect.

Signs

Can temporary signs, traffic cones etc. be used to assist.

Communication

Utilise CCTV cameras and control room support to assist, monitor and implement counter measures. Update control and colleagues throughout. Communicate requests for additional officers and equipment if needed.

Vehicles

If vehicles are involved record details:

- Number of vehicles involved / Type / Colour / License number
- Direction of travel and speed prior to collision
- Condition and damage to vehicles
- Note any body contact and paint transfer details
- Hazards in vehicle (including anything incriminating)

People

- Identify driver and occupants and request details
- Demeanour of occupants
- Condition of occupants:

  a) Trapped
  b) Injured
  c) Suffering illness
  d) Intoxicated
  e) In need of first aid or emergency services

- Can they understand you / are they fully alert
- Request personal details
- Request statement of account from all involved
- Obtain witness statements and names of 3rd party witness's

A.C.E.C.A.R.D ASSESSMENT STEPS

1) APPROACH
2) CAUTION SIGNS
3) EXAMINE SCENE
4) CASUALTIES
5) AMBULANCE (OTHER EMERGENCY SERVICES)
6) REMOVAL
7) DETAILS

Approach the scene, implement "SAFER" consider dangers to yourself and others.

Caution Signs cones and support vehicles, can they be used to redirect and reduce further risk or danger.

Examine the scene (assess what has happened in order to best respond).

Casualties, provide first aid response if required (offer).

Ambulance or other required responders.

Removal of hazard return to continuity if possible (only to be done if no accident/crime is involved).

Details of event/incident, those involved, witness's etc.

Vehicle Hazard Information Plates

As a means of controlling access and safety on any site you must be aware of all maintenance and service vehicles permitted to enter, including those which may affect safety and the content of those vehicles in order to assess their need for permission to enter. Vehicles carrying hazardous material must display information plates to identify the product contained within and the risks it may pose to the environment if the substance is not handled and controlled correctly.

Hazard Warning Indicator Sign

Initial observations should be drawn to the hazard warning indicator sign. This is the best way to immediately and quickly assess the risk in relation to the product, and this is conveniently placed in a diamond figure. The numbers relate to the specific product and hazard posed.

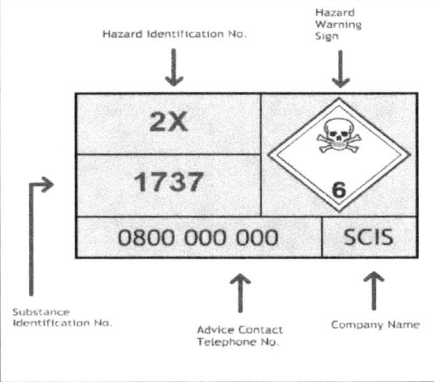

This information should be recorded as part of your access control and monitoring system. Any site which permits access for vehicles containing hazardous material must do so in line with all health and safety legislation and codes of practice for safety contained within:

(COSHH) Control Of Substances Hazardous to Health.

Visit : www.hse.gov.uk/coshh

However regardless of whether a person is based at a commercial or industrial complex where vehicles containing hazardous material are routinely permitted or not, it is advisable that all have a basic understanding of these plates and pro-actively observe them on approaching vehicles. As in any emergency situation information is king. You may come across as a result of an RTC (Road Traffic Collision) a tanker and as part of your risk assessment in order to proceed you may need to understand the content in relation to the risk. This information can also be relayed to any responding emergency services in order for them to advise and formulate their response.

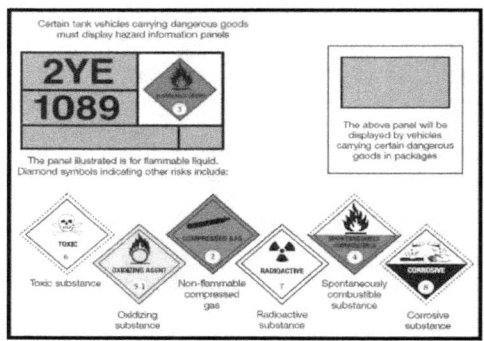

Emergency Vehicle Access

This is often a consideration which is overlooked. We spend much of our time focusing on fire and emergency regulations which impact our ability to run a business but seem to overlook the application operationally. If you are working at a location that attracts large numbers of visitors having a poorly implemented plan in regard to parking layout can soon overwhelm the site, resulting in delays and hindered access for the emergency services. Therefore regular foot patrols and routine CCTV camera patrols of access routes and parking facilities should be utilised to maintain route safety. Delays can cause fatalities.

Allowing vehicles to park on grass verges or in precarious locations may seem the easy option in allowing immediate customer satisfaction and avoiding aggression from the public. But the easy option is not always the best option and the greater customer service concern is the preservation of life. Therefore if a parked vehicle does not allow for a vehicle as wide as a fire appliance to successfully negotiate or have access then move it on.

Hazard /Obstruction

Different types of highway and conditions require different responses. High speed traffic behaves differently than traffic at lower speeds and assessment risks, although including many of the same consideration, are higher on roads with greater speed limits. As stated earlier our traffic management duties are confined to privately maintained land and retail and commercial environments, therefore we are only considering operations within a 30mph zone or lower and we will consider dealing with flow and obstructions to highway in this type of location only.

Our priority when it comes to any obstruction on the highway or footpath is promoting a safe environment, and to reduce the impact and risk to the public. Whether you are dealing with a vehicle obstruction or debris the risk is the same. It is our job to reduce the impact of the incident and remove further dangers.

All hazards must be reported and dealt with immediately. If repairs are not possible straight away you should assess the risk and impact of the hazard and do all that is reasonably possible to reduce not only the impact on pedestrian and traffic flow but the increased risk of injury. Your employer is liable therefore it is your duty to respond, make the area safe or alert those at risk.

Make others aware of the hazard with the addition of traffic cones marking the area. We do this in order to provide ample warning to road users of the upcoming danger in order to avoid it. These avoidance measures work in conjunction with our actions and our support structures in order to reduce the impact of the event and the knock on effect on the environment.

Consider a road traffic hazard with a birds eye view to the approach. Cones, signs and markings should give ample warning of the upcoming danger and guide vehicles away. Abrupt close proximity signs and markings do not forewarn motorists of the risk and increase the chance of creating a bottle neck and congestion.

Response Vehicles

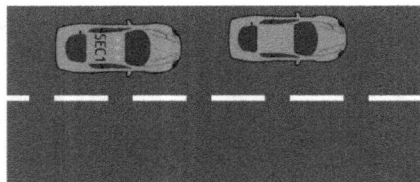 

If you have marked response vehicles available for use, they should approach the scene with hazard warning beacons flashing. Park with the flow of traffic blocking the hazard and acting as protection towards any public in that location, while at the same time warning and dispersing vehicles that approach.

In order to mark out a hazard where possible we should use emergency signs in order to re-route traffic safely. But the immediate hazard should be marked out not only for traffic but also with pedestrians in mind and officers utilised in place to advise, assist and respond to any concerns. Whether the obstacle is debris such as a fallen tree or a road traffic collision, the lay out principle of cones should be done in line with the speed and flow of the traffic in that environment. We are primarily working in locations where the maximum speed allowed is 30mph, therefore warning cones should be placed alerting oncoming vehicles starting at a minimum distance of 50 metres from the obstacle concerned.

In an ideal world access to signs and cones would be unlimited however in reality obtaining the ideal amount is either not possible or only available after an extensive search period. Therefore lay out what you do have available, report any deficiencies, and utilise officers in high visibility clothing to alert other road users.

CHAPTER TWELVE
Fire Precautions

A security officer is also a fire marshal, and it is advisable if you don't have any knowledge, experience or confidence regarding fire safety and the use of fire fighting equipment that you either attend a course or approach your employer. It is not only something that you can add to your CV it saves lives. If you work for an employer permanently based at a venue then you should as a matter of course undergo during induction some form of training in relation to dealing with a fire activation. If your duties are to provide security and safety for the premises then training in the use of extinguishers and other fire fighting equipment held on site should be included. You must be aware of risks and procedures, building and site layout, muster points and evacuation.

This chapter provides awareness of fire precautions and fire fighting equipment available in the workplace. It is not designed to replace professional and practically applied training. It is the responsibility of all staff members to understand the evacuation procedures where they work and it is the duty of the company to provide all means necessary within their legal obligation to train their staff in order to comply with all legislation.

The Workplace

Fire alarms and other equipment should be regularly tested. You must be able to demonstrate a working knowledge of this equipment, be aware and confident that all material both technical and practical used to either prevent, alert or tackle a fire is in full working order. Your workplace has a duty of care to all employees and visitors and in order to maintain this, emergency procedures must be drilled regularly. Knowing your workplace is easier if you are continually stationed in one location. If you are only working security in a building for one day it may seem unimportant to know the layout and hard to remember but security is there to provide safety. And first and foremost safety for yourself. Therefore no matter how difficult or unimportant you may find it you should be confirming deployment details and location procedures and information prior to taking up any operation at any given location. Having all the answers is not always possible especially when working in a new or unfamiliar location. You should however have a good communication network, allowing you to ask and get the right answers.

Fire Marshal Duties

A security officer based at a site or venue carries out regular security patrols. Therefore it makes logical sense that part of the role is to act as a fire marshal. Routine and periodic visual inspection of internal and external areas allows for the timely reporting of hazards and concerns.

SECURITY = SAFETY

On Patrol Check list

- Exit doors are in working order and free from obstruction
- Escape routes clear/free of combustibles
- Damage to building fabric (damage hinders containment)
- Fire safety signs correct and in place
- Fire call points unobstructed
- Fire extinguishers in place and full with seals intact
- Fire doors closed and functioning
- Emergency lighting and equipment in working order
- Fire alarm tested
- Faults reported and paperwork completed

Procedure

Fire action

Any person on discovering a fire should

1) Sound the alarm
2) Phone in-house emergency number or Fire Service 999
3) Attack the fire using appliances provided if possible.

On hearing a fire alarm activation

4) Leave the building by fire evacuation routes
5) Close all doors behind yourselves
6) Report to assembly point

The above is the standard evacuation procedure in the event of a fire emergency.
As a security professional you may and will be tasked in the evacuation and monitoring of the situation as a immediate action response to the threat of fire.

Fire Point

The above is an example of a fire point, they are located on passageways and exit routes and should be on each level of the building. They give clear procedural instructions and provide access to fire fighting material such as extinguishers.

Extinguishers

The correct extinguisher should always be used on the correct type of fire. The style of extinguisher used within the building should be installed with consideration taken to the purpose of the building and type of flammable goods held on the premises.

Prior to European Union interference extinguishers were fully colour coded in relation to their content, meaning a CO_2 extinguisher was all black in colour and a H_2O (water) one was red. Some would say this made them more obvious in an emergency but now in a case of creating uniformity they are all red in colour distinguishable by colour coded label plates.

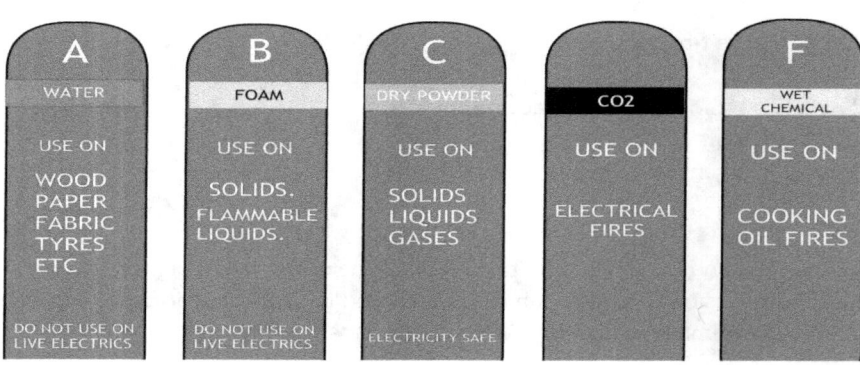

Choosing the correct extinguisher

A	WATER	RED	Class A fires: Fires involving freely burning materials. (wood, paper, textiles etc.)
B	FOAM	CREAM	Class A + B fires: Can be used on class A fires and also (Flammable liquids and spirits) NOT SUITABLE FOR ALCOHOL / COOKING OILS
C	DRY POWDER	BLUE	Class C, can also be used on Class A and B (Flammable gases, butane and propane)
	CO2 CARBON DIOXIDE	BLACK	Can be used on Class B fires, suitable for use on domestic electrical appliances
F	WET CHEMICAL	YELLOW	Can be used on all Class of fire, and fires involving cooking oils and fat

Each extinguisher should be security tagged, with a pressure display which alerts you to whether or not it is full. You must pay attention to this equipment whilst on patrol in order to check the items are in working order and have not been tampered with. Any damaged or broken tags or low pressure extinguishers should be reported and replaced immediately.

Hydrants

Hydrants are standpipe connections placed in external locations in order for the attending fire service to utilize the water supply to tackle fires in that location. They are visibly situated in the public street and also on large private commercial sites. It is wise to familiarise yourself with the locations of hydrants within your companies domain as this information will be needed by any attending fire crew.

Hydrant locations are identifiable by plates which consist of a yellow background with a large black H indicating hydrant. The size of the hydrant and distance from the plate is indicated by the numbers on the plate itself.

Diameter of Hydrant in Milimetres.

Distance of Hydrant from plate in Metres.

All modern hydrants are labelled in metric however you will still find some imperial ones if you look hard enough.

This style of plate indicates that the hydrant at that location is a double hydrant meaning two standpipes can be attached.

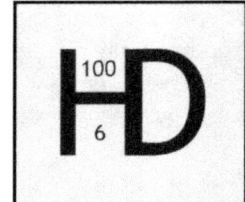

Fire Alarm Panels

Fire alarm panels come in many different shapes and sizes depending on the use of the premises they cover. Some integrated systems work from a main control board operated from a CCTV or management hub, often with slave boards situated to provide alert information at locations around the site. Other smaller sites such as shops and offices may work from a single panel. Whichever is used the principle of identifying the reason why the panel has activated is the same.

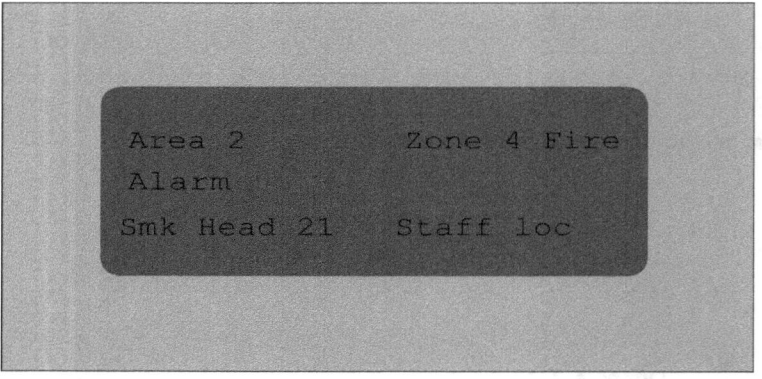

Heads up Digital Display

Knowing what to do, where to look and how to respond saves time, money but most of all lives.

The heads up display will indicate the cause of activation. It is therefore vital that those tasked with safety understand how the fire system works and how the panel information relates to the layout of the building and the workings of all sensors and alarms. It is also vital that staff are drilled in operational procedures, especially in roles which involve services to the public and sales. It is often a compelling action to silence or re-set, as the auditory alarm is off-putting to customers or staff, believing and sometimes hoping the system is in fault. This occurs more often than you would think especially in the retail sector, silencing a system in favour of benefiting trade at the risk of public safety. However doing so without carrying out inspection and understanding the information provided by the panel while it is in fire and by clearing this information which becomes automatic once the panel is re-set means you cannot fully assess the cause. Doing so not only affects your insurance liability but your legal and operational obligations. This point is being made because a security officer has a duty of care. You may find yourself in the situation of responding to an alarm or being employed by a company which routinely re-sets a panel they believe to be acting up. You may consider this as the responsibility of the site manager and not something you need to concern yourself with. Complacency is a killer, a security professional knows that it is their duty to understand the risks and raise concerns. Remember commercial buildings and structures may have recesses and voids which may be monitored electronically and not easily visible or accessible therefore every activation must be taken seriously and acted on.

"Training is the key ingredient for handling disaster"

Walter Maddox

Wet/Dry Risers

Multi-storey buildings will contain risers to assist the fire service by providing water pressure throughout the building allowing for the attachment of fire hoses. As the name suggests a wet riser is one that is pressurised with water where as a dry riser is not. Knowing the location and type of riser inside the building will greatly help responding fire fighters.

Fire Fighter Staircase

These are staircases which are pressurised in order to repel smoke and are used by responding fire-fighters as a staging point to tackle the fire. Responding fire appliances should be directed where possible to these locations.

Break Glass Units

KNOWING THE DIFFERENCE

Break the glass to activate the fire alarm
Fire system cannot be re-set till break glass
unit repaired and glass panel replaced.

This unit is found close to security controlled doors
as a over ride in the event of an emergency It is not
connected to a fire alarm system.
The glass must be replaced and the unit re-set in
order to re-secure the door therefore these items
should be inspected periodically.

Communication

For obvious reasons in any emergency rapid communication is needed, whether to alert
and arrange responders or in the event of a false alarm stand them down.

Establish and transmit cause. *"No Smoke No Fire, cause of activation is"* (x) or to
the contrary if needed.

Fire Service

There should be procedures in place to facilitate the arrival of the fire service in order to
assist them as much as possible. Having a pre-arranged muster point for arriving fire
crews is preferable for large companies. But establishing excellent lines of communication
and updated information is a must regardless of building size and occupancy.

CHAPTER THIRTEEN
Retail Security

Retail crime costs the UK economy millions each year. You will often hear alleged offenders declaring it as a victimless crime, attempting to disassociate these types of offences from the mainstream. Often blaming faceless corporations for facilitating the opportunity, as if they are committing some form of moral justice. This is either a misguided illusion or a blatant attempt at deflection. If you have ever arrested a person for theft you have probably heard all the excuses and reasoning.

There is no excuse for illegally appropriating the goods of another, whether from an individual or a business. Retail crime has much wider ramifications, it affects the cost of goods, increases insurance premiums and affects the livelihood of the business owner which often has a knock on effect for the staff.

Centre for Retail Research - Financial cost of Retail Crime 2012 – 13

Customer Theft	£2,206 million	+ 2.8%
Employee Theft/Fraud	£1,681 million	- 4.8%
Supplier/Warehouse fraud	£ 246 million	+ 28.8%
Card Fraud	£ 85 million	- 29.2%
Robbery/Burglary	£ 120 million	+ 5.3%
Criminal Damage	£ 81 million	+ 24.6%
Cyber Fraud	£ 280 million	+ 6.8%
Security and loss prevention	£ 995 million	- 2.4%
Total	£5,694 million	+ 4.9%

The total demonstrates the financial cost, including the cost of applied counter-measures to the retail sector.

Preventing Retail Crime

Preventing retail crime is not just the responsibility of the business owner, or the security staff. It is the responsibility of every agent employed by the company from store manager to shop assistant.

Minimise that Risk!

DON'T

- Keep small easily accessible untagged items by entrances.

- Leave the shop floor free of staff

- Lay out your stock or building fabric in such a fashion that visibility is restricted.

DO

- Maintain good lighting throughout the store.

- Visible CCTV (Deterrent)

- Place CCTV cameras with stock and layout in mind, avoid blind spots

- Train staff to monitor customers

- Use uniformed guards (Deterrent)

- Utilise plain clothes store detectives to monitor, assist and collect evidence.

CCTV

Utilise CCTV to monitor customers and staff on premises. The placement of these cameras must be done with consideration taken as to the layout of the floor space and stock. All too often cameras are placed in a first fix style, meaning they work well covering an open plan area wall to wall but are not re-positioned or reassessed in relation to additional building fabric once racks rails and stock is added.
Remember you should always be aiming to achieve continuity of evidence and we do this by maintaining line of site which includes video evidence. Loss of vision creates doubt and can risk securing a conviction. CCTV only works if it is monitored and reviewed, and its efficacy periodically tested. Maintaining fixed camera positions on entrances and exits provides excellent evidence.

Staff Placement & Customer Service

The best deterrent for any shoplifter is observational staff. One excellent placement for a staff member is at the entrance, not only as a means of welcoming customers but it also has a psychological effect on those wishing to steal, as it reinforces the belief that they are being monitored as soon as they enter the store. They will also be aware that they will have to pass this person again in order to get away as they are blocking their escape. Therefore in the guise of offering outstanding customer service by welcoming people and by providing assistance to those in store, you are actively deterring crime.

Shoplifters

When it comes to shoplifters there is no specific type, no particular style of dress or identifying attributes. Anybody could be a shoplifter, smartly dressed, casual or dishevelled. All have the opportunity and any person can possess the will to do so. A shoplifter may act alone or as part of a group, it could be a impulsive action or a premeditated act.

Offender Types

Juvenile

operating either alone or in groups, sometimes as a result of peer pressure. Often seeing the law as a challenge rather than something to adhere to, often believing that their youth somehow excuses them from responsibility.

Impulse

A person that doesn't go out with the purpose or intent to shoplift. This group can consist of those which you would consider "respectable" in background. You can counter the impulse shoplifter by concentrating on prevention, training staff, moving stock and layout.

Kleptomania

Those with a psychological compulsion to steal, often stealing not for monetary value or usefulness of the item.

Addiction

This group are often identifiable by attitude and dress, combining that with their addiction compels them to take greater risk during the theft. This often makes them easier to spot but harder to read. This group can be volatile when stopped and should be handled with caution. (although caution should be used in all cases)

Professional

A professional although this term may seem to give false legitimacy to their actions, either working alone or in a team they are highly adept and often difficult to spot. Stealing items either to order or those which are popular and easy to offload, regularly concentrating on small high value items.

How they do it

Sometimes quietly working alone sometimes in groups or teams, either to distract the attention of others or to facilitate a heavier hit. I have worked in locations where three suspected shoplifters have been identified only to discover they were part of a team of 20 which were all operating at the venue at the same time. I have also seen prams being used not only to carry a baby, the list could go on......

The Complacent Officer

Complacency is dangerous, and routine breeds complacency. No arrest or interaction with a suspected offender should ever be considered routine. This is worth remembering for all situations but to use a retail stop or arrest works as a good example. The simplest routine answer or situation is not always correct. You see a product, you see the offender you witness the crime, you initiate the stop. A simple routine exercise?. The complacency is compounded by the low value of the item stolen, or the size or demeanour of the perpetrator. But you must remember you do not know this person and your assumptions regarding the situation may be misguided. You never know how they are going to react, you don't know their background and you don't know what other issues may be involved. This person may just be an opportunist grabbing a £30 item of stock as they leave but it is also possible that this same person has recently committed a more serious offence and is wanted on warrant. This results in them feeling more inclined to flee at any cost and by you hindering that objective you may end up being the victim of their desperation. This has not been said in order to instil fear. It is to make you aware and make you think and consider the possibilities and understand the importance of taking tactical control of all stops and arrests.

Retail Crime Initiative (RCI)

Many towns, cities and shopping centre complexes actively promote regional/area RCI's. They operate in order to bring together business and police to share intelligence and work together to prevent, disrupt and deter those who are intent on committing retail crime.

BENEFITS:

Brings retailers, the police and local authority together.

Shares intelligence on prolific offenders and crime trends.

Combines and focusses resources.

Closer operational support between retailers.

Allows for implementation of exclusion orders effective in all member stores.

Shop Watch

A shop watch service connects differing stores together with local CCTV. Connecting communications allows for the passing of information in real time to all stores and agencies. It is extremely beneficial in gathering evidence regarding the movement and actions of suspects, fore warning other shops in the area in relation to a crime or emergency.

Intelligence/Evidence gathering

Intelligence and evidence dictates how we deal with those we suspect of criminality. Intelligence may be received by a customer alerting you or information given to you by other stores, staff or the police. For example during a RCI meeting details are shared regarding a particular offender operating in the area. This person has now entered your store, acting on this intelligence you monitor throughout in order to gather evidence on that offender in relation to their activities or in order to secure an arrest or provide updated intelligence.

S.C.O.N.E

The SCONE principle facilitates a fluid approach to dealing with those suspected of retail theft. It provides a process of relevant steps in order to facilitate a positive outcome. There is now a general consensus that an "A" is placed at the beginning making it ASCONE, the "A" standing for APPROACH referring to the period where the suspect is being watched as they make their approach towards the item before picking it up. The reasoning for this addition may be sound but in reality rather unnecessary. A far better word to incorporate would be CONTINUITY, especially in the form of observation, If you do not maintain this throughout then all the other points fall apart.

SCONE meaning:

Selection, the process of selecting an item

Concealment, the suspect conceals the item on their person, in their bag etc.

Observational CONTINUITY, maintain this throughout, via clear line of site or by CCTV to confirm items remain in their possession and have not been discarded

Non payment, the suspect makes no attempt to pay, passing by pay points

Exit, the suspect exits or is attempting to exit

At this point you can now approach the suspect and question them on suspicion of theft. You have every legal right to approach someone and if necessary arrest them on suspicion of committing an indictable offence. However if we stick to and act on the SCONE principle maintaining OBSERVATIONAL CONTINUITY throughout we can ensure our actions are sound and any subsequent prosecution safe.

EVIDENCE FACILITATES ACTION !

Observational Alarm Bells

As stated any person could be a shoplifter, no matter their age, status, race, religion or sex. Certain things however should arouse suspicion and facilitate further investigation and observation.

Clothing

Are they wearing unseasonal clothing, large jackets, baggy or bulky with multiple pockets, does their clothing have smooth lines, does the clothing look altered.

Attitude

Is a customer using distraction techniques to pre-occupy staff while others commit the theft. Is a customer excessively interested in staff positioning, are they observing the activity of security and staff members. Are they over visually scanning the premises. Are they spending an excessive amount of time in one location, whilst maintaining a view or line of sight towards the exit. These are just a few things which could indicate an offender risk. They may also be innocent actions of a shopper. But any suspicions should warrant covert monitoring.

Baggage

Are they carrying a bag in an easily accessible manner. Is the bag large, has it been modified in any way (such as foil lined).

Plastic branded bags

Are they carrying a branded plastic bag from a unknown or distant store (a non local store or a brand which is not sold in commutable distance) does the bag look worn and well used, this is more likely since the advent of charging for bags but it could indicate that the bag has been modified to block electronic tagging devices.

Gift Bags

Gift bags are a popular item, they are sturdy but also easy to modify. They hold their shape more easily therefore it is harder to tell when they are full. They may be often bright and noticeable in colour but this does not seem to put people off using them. The large sturdy opening at the top allows for quick and easy access, often bright in colour but rarely branded which means they can be modified and taken to any store without suspicion. These bags can sometimes be enormous, therefore pay close attention if someone enters with one of these. The bonus of their sturdy design means the opening at the top can be scanned and looked in by a store detective as they covertly pass by or by a competent CCTV operator. To combat this many shoplifters will refrain from using the handles in favour of holding the bag closed physically or rolling the top over, and those carrying a gift bag in this fashion should be heavily monitored. Many stores have taken to stapling the top closed after purchasing a gift bagged item, putting the bag out of use for covert shoplifting means. A newly purchased gift bag would be clean and look new, if it looks older, has folds as though it has been stored prior to use then alarm bells should be ringing.

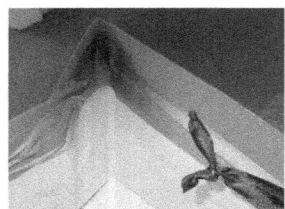

Covertly foil lined – The foil has been overlaid with another bag in an attempt to avoid visual detection.

SUSPICION + EVIDENCE = ACTION

Going equipped

Going equipped to steal is an offence within itself.

Items which retail offenders may carry

- Modified bags
- Knives/blades , cutters etc. to remove tags
- Additional foil
- De-tagging devices

This is by no means an extensive list. There are probably many more items they can use and as technology moves to combat this issue offenders soon catch up with devices to counter them. It is purely to demonstrate the principle of going equipped but also remind any arresting officer of the need to approach with caution.

Tags & Countermeasures

RF (Radio Frequency) Product anti shoplifting alarms are often placed either side of public entrance in order to react/activate via sensors within the product tag when proximity is detected. Depending on the product and the particular tag used the tag/countermeasure would either be deactivated or removed at point of purchase.

Have you ever been in a store and on exiting heard the alarm sound? Whether a false alarm or an act of theft it should always be acted upon, possibly a person has innocently purchased an item and the tag had not been de-activated. In this case the customer should alert the staff to check their items as getting home and finding a tag especially on an item of clothing means returning to the store to have it removed or trying yourself and damaging your purchase.

This is another reason staff should be placed at the entrance to assist if the alarm sounds, innocent customers will often stop whereas an offender will keep moving. Either way an alarm should draw your attention and arouse your suspicions. However more often than not the alarm will sound and no response is offered by the store staff, this negates any value of the countermeasure. You can put items in place but if the staff do not react then you have wasted your money. Next time you go shopping take a look around if you hear one of these alarms sound, and see if any staff members takes notice, especially if they have a uniform marked security.

Tags come in all shapes and sizes, some overt and others covert to avoid detection by a shoplifter. Applying tags to goods is often a value driven exercise and for that reason it is advisable to not keep low value untagged items close to the doors. Shoplifters are often opportunists so don't tempt them.

Overt (Ink) Security tag

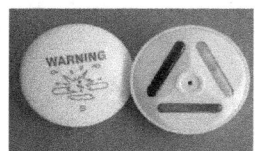

Radio frequency tags

These are just a few of the tag styles available

Retail Changing Rooms

Changing rooms can often be used to conceal items prior to exit. Minimise the risk by placing a member of staff to supervise their use.

Supervising staff should

- Control and monitor the area
- Limit the number of people permitted at one time
- Implement a limit of items allowed per visit
- Count number of items taken in and confirm on leaving
- Inspect changing rooms before and after each use (confirm area sterile)
- Report any concerns/suspicions

Clothing Rails

When it comes to retail clothing outlets, they like any other sales platform rightly choose a lay out of product that is both neat and appealing to the purchasing public.
In doing so they also make it easier for those wishing to steal the items on display. A common error when hanging clothing on display rails is to place all the hangers facing the same direction.

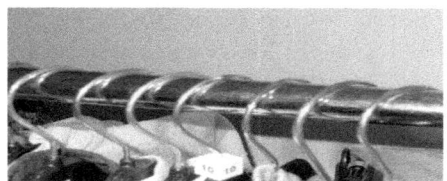

This may be appealing to the eye but this uniformity not only allows for customers to remove clothing , it allows shoplifters to carry out bulk theft with ease. It not only makes it easier and quicker for the lone shoplifter to remove a large volume in one go, but also for a well disciplined team to hit using shock and ore tactics, grab in bulk and make off with thousands of pounds worth of merchandise. It may be wise to weigh the cosmetic appeal against the risk before laying items out in this fashion or at least if you wish to maintain a uniform appeal to your hanging policy don't implement it for stock that is hung close to the entrances.

Prosecution

When it comes to prosecution some stores seem reluctant to prosecute those suspected of theft. This may be due to fears of being sued or concerns regarding their brand image. It could even be to avoid the hassle, or as a concern regarding staff competence.
Whatever the reason the risks of not prosecuting must be considered and ultimately understood. Failing to prosecute or being seen as an easy target increases the rate of offending, word spreads and more come. When more come you not only increase stock loss but increase the risk, especially towards staff and even customers should they choose to intervene. It also brings into question why you are employing security staff. If it is purely to observe and deter then that can be done by CCTV cameras and big signs.
If you are afraid that your security is not competent to deal with arrests, then I suggest you re-evaluate your ability to employ staff because you need to replace them with professionals.

CHAPTER FOURTEEN
The Venue

When it comes to securing a venue the security procedures and objectives may be the same but the level of response will be dependent on the use of the premises, the clientèle and background of those that are permitted to enter and the purpose and objectives to be achieved. Although the same principles apply. The implementation for a corporate office complex would for obvious reasons differ from that of a retail or leisure venue. A thorough and robust risk and threat assessment must always be carried out. For this chapter we will be considering those locations that allow public access to one degree or another. We will consider how the site is used and the corporate responsibility for safety and customer service towards those that enter with the permission of the owners.
This includes; staff, contractors and the general public at large. Security is not just a legal requirement or a means of detecting or deterring unlawful acts. It facilitates the smooth operation of any site by understanding the needs and requirements of that site and facilitating their implementation. From controlling access and movement, to covertly and overtly monitoring for threat and concerns for safety. The security department or team allows those that use that location, either as a visitor or as a base for running a business or service, to do so with minimum disruption.

Base of Operations (Security Staff)

The entire venue is your base of operations. Regardless of your particular duty, you may be tasked in one location to carry out one particular role at a given time but you are one link in a very large chain. Your duties link to that of your colleagues and are organised by your deployment centre or control room. Any intended or unintended failings of the individual puts not only the objectives of the business at risk but the safety and security of all those on site.

Considerations

- Risk / Threat assessment
- Customer Service
- Site safety and security
- Operational concerns
- Access (Customers, staff, contractors and suppliers)
- First Aid and emergency provisions

Control

Regardless of the size of venue a good command and control structure must be instilled in order to promote fluidity towards your goal of minimising risk and promoting success. Whether this comes in the form of a well maintained CCTV control room, monitoring site activity and deployment, or it is something as make shift as a tent or even a single person point of contact. All actions must be controlled, recorded and understood. If we don't know what people are doing or what is needed we cannot provide a professional service.

Overview

All security personnel on site must be aware of site layout in regard to security operations, understanding access, routes, positions and locations speeds up your response.
For a small location this can be an easy task however a robust site may take time to understand and this is where excellent support and communication comes in.

Site Assessment

As a private contractor your duties often terminate at the perimeter of the site. Being aware of the property boundary is often in your best interest, not just for your safety but also for insurance purposes. The boundary represents a distinction between operational and non operational locations. However this does not mean you always stop at it, it is just an awareness of the risk in order for YOU !! as an individual to assess. Use common sense and cross it only if it is necessary operationally and you have justification to do so. It is one thing responding and chasing down an offender onto the public highway but if that leaves limited personnel putting the site at further risk then by getting carried away with the chase means you are failing in you primary role. Understand the boundary and put in place countermeasures to defend it. Whether this includes fences and gates, again will be determined by the objectives of the location. Prisons have walls and gates for a reason. A shopping or convention centre built to the same specifications would not be wise nor welcoming.

Therefore it could be something as simple as a tree-line marking the perimeter or in some cases nothing at all. Regardless of the physical or non-physical barrier you as a security provider should visualize a perimeter, understand the control needs and working backwards from the outer point, apply security measures inwards towards the centre base of operations.

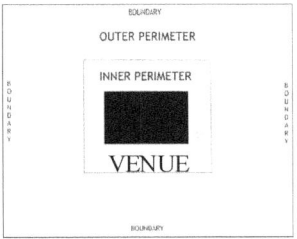

Outer perimeter / zone

This may consist of fences and gates with access and control measures. The perimeter should be monitored by CCTV and roaming patrols and static positioning with mobile vehicle support response if available.

Inner perimeter (on – site)

Regular camera patrols promoting safety and a visible uniformed presence adds to deter as well as defend.

Site Control

The security department/team have to be in control of the site. They must have a 360 degree vision of the entire location. All activity by those on site must be monitored and recorded. The system cannot react if it is not aware. Security should always work hand in glove with the site management, failing to inform or pass intelligence to a security detail puts security operations and objectives at risk.

Access (Operational Worker / Business Activity)

All sites require access, whether they be for public or private use. Access should be provided in a safe and secure manner, areas restricted should be secured and kept sterile in line with promoting safety. Considerations must be made for all safety and fire regulations and staff employed on site must be trained to deal with site activity.
All contractors and suppliers must only have access to those areas which are needed to carry out their work. Their details and reasons for entering the site must be known and they must be supervised and monitored throughout. Whether that be by continued physical supervision or by remote camera patrols. All visitors must be logged and timings recorded.

Check for

- Structural & foreign object hazards
- Damage/hazards to building fabric
- Public access areas are open and clear
- Security & restricted areas are secure

Public Attraction

If the site is customer service focused and the layout and design is put in place in order to attract and welcome members of the public, all restricted access locations should be maintained in line with this. Unsecured access to restricted areas puts your business at risk. Areas such as service corridors and maintenance yards are dangerous locations, uncontrolled access is a danger to the public and also allows those with criminal motives to enter.

Vehicle Access (restrictions)

Public customer parking should always be covertly monitored by roaming and static CCTV surveillance. Utilizing traffic management officers/external security staff provides good customer service and reassurance to the public.

Any access for vehicles to restricted areas or closed locations and sites should be heavily controlled, prior knowledge by the security team regarding vehicles wanting to come on site allows for greater access control. If vehicle arrival times can be arranged with visitors and contractors it will speed up the process and avoid the risk of the system being overwhelmed and procedures being compromised. It is understandable that this is not always possible but if this can be done it works as a benefit to all.

Vehicles Entering Restricted Areas

Record Details;

- Driver ID
- Vehicle: make, model, colour and registration
- TOA (Time of Arrival)
- Reason and destination
- Load & vehicle visibly inspected/searched
- TOD (Time of Departure)

Patrolling

For the security officer tasked to patrol they are not only operating as a visual representation of their employer but also of themselves and the industry at large.
You should also be aware you are a brand in your own right. Patrolling means just that,

being on patrol. In other words moving around. If you are tasked to do this and you are not mobile then you are putting others at risk. The venue should be broken down into zones and patrol officers dispersed to cover each of them. This optimizes a 360 degree presence.

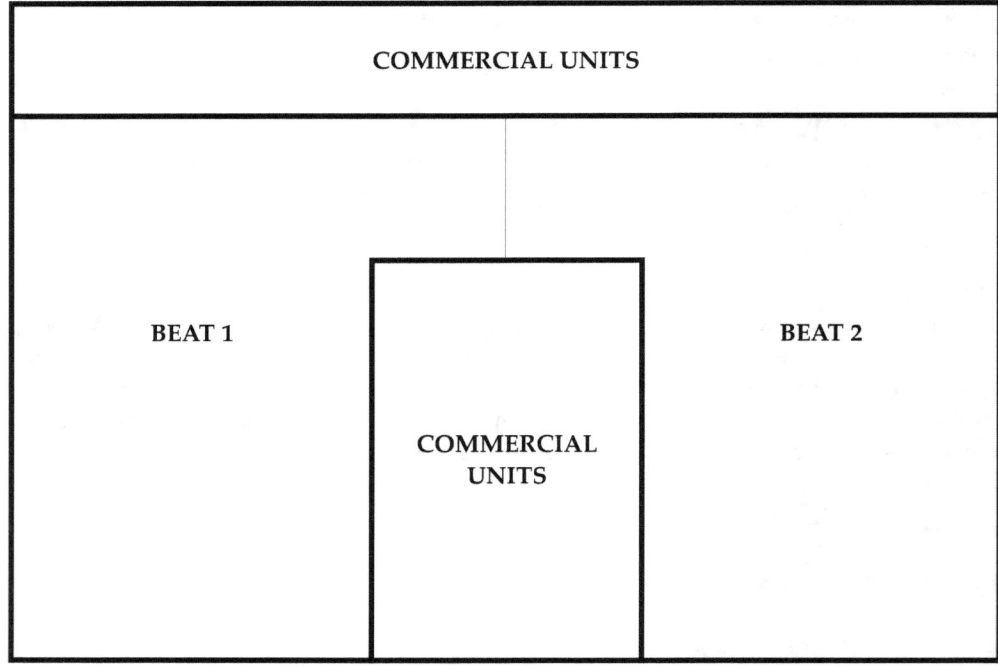

DESIGNATED BEATS ALLOW FOR OPERATIONAL CONTROL
AND OPTIMAL COVERAGE

Pre-deployment briefing should identify your role and objectives and location of operation.

Patrolling Objectives

- Minimise risk
- To visibly deter crime and anti-social behaviour
- Provide Customer Service assistance
- Respond to and investigate incidents
- To assist

- Reduce disorder
- Provide or facilitate first aid and emergency response

First Aid / Medical Provisions

It is good business practice and in some cases a legal requirement to provide first aid cover depending on the type of venue you are operating. It is also wise that those working in the industry do hold some form of medical qualification and operational experience.

One problem which often occurs is that even when people do receive training, depending on where they work they rarely get the chance to use it. It is also wise to remember that some, even though they hold a qualification, for whatever reason feel unable to, or lack the confidence to, as an individual provide medical provision. Those that feel this way should inform their employer or team and either increase their training or accept their limitations. That way the provision of service can be addressed. It is not something that a operator can wing or bluff their way through. Speaking from my own personal experience, having been through extensive periods where my medical skills were not called into action, then moving into an environment where they were called upon daily was initially a daunting experience. It is not just worthwhile to maintain your renewal training, you must gain as much operational experience as possible.

Providing on site medical equipment speeds up response times and can often be life-saving. Having that kit well maintained and regularly inspected and accessible and combining that with well trained users is a big tick against the customer service box.

Public Houses / Nightclub Door Staff

Hospitality venue door staff are able to act under the provisions laid out in the Licensing act.

Licensing Act 2003:Failure to leave licensed premises

The licensing act 2003 Chapter 17 Part 7 Section 143 covers duties of the licensee and their agents/door supervisors in relation to admission and ejection of persons from licensed premises.

1)   A person who is drunk or disorderly commits an offence if, without reasonable excuse-

> a) Fails to leave relevant premises when requested by a constable or by a person to whom subsection (2) applies, or
>
> b) he enters or attempts to enter relevant premises after a constable or a person to whom subsection (2) has requested him not to enter.

2)   This subsection applies -

> a) To any person who works at the premises in a capacity, whether paid or unpaid which authorises him to make such a request.
>
> b) In the case of licensed premises to -
>
>> (i) The holder of a premises licence in respect of the premises, or
>>
>> (ii) The designated premises supervisor (if any) under such a licence,
>
> c) In the case of premise in respect of which a club premises certificate has effect, to any member or officer of the club which holds the certificate who is present on the premises in a capacity which enables him to make such a request, and
>
> d) In the case of premises which may be used for a permitted temporary activity by virtue of part 5, to the premises user in relation to the temporary event notice in question.

3)   A person guilty of an offence under subsection (1) is liable on summary conviction to a fine not exceeding level 1 on the standard scale.

4)   On being requested to do so by a person to whom subsection (2) applies, a constable must -

a) help to expel from relevant premises a person who is drunk or disorderly

b) help to prevent such a person from entering relevant premises

Staff employed to provide a security presence within licensed premises utilise the provisions within the Licensing Act 2003 in order to control the access and use of the premises by its patrons and by their actions promote a safe environment.

As with all premises door staff are employed to enforce conditions of entry, maintain order and eject those which fail to comply with the legislation.

One Man Doors

Taking into consideration all that has been previously outlined and now having risk assessed the role, it is logical to surmise that no security officer working in a high risk environment should be doing so alone. This is a serious issue and should be treated as such. Any so called security company which would even consider sending one person to a pub or club puts that person and the patrons and business at risk. One member of door staff has no practical application. It increases risk of injury to that doorman and also to the public. One person trying to remove another cannot do so in a safe manner. It is not the old days where working the "doors" was expected to be a demonstration of your strength. Nor should any hostile interaction with members of the public end up from the outset an issue of self defence, which if you are working alone it will often become.

You have to follow the law and only carry out actions which you can justify. Being licensed means you should be able to risk assess the situation, and if events unfold which lead to the question being asked as to why the security response was inadequate and resulted in greater harm or injury, how can a security provider justify their provision. The same questions should and will be asked of the individual, any person who is prepared to stand in a bar or on a door, is being asked to provide security and they need to understand the duties they are undertaking. You are either there merely to observe events, something any person who is in the building could do or you are there to; and are prepared to act which is something you cannot do lawfully and safely as a lone worker in a high risk licensed environment. If you fail to value this point and are willing to do so, be prepared to be either assaulted or arrested.

1 – 100 principle

You may hear this phrase a lot. It is bandied around in the industry to reflect a misguided attitude towards staff deployment. It is considered for insurance purposes only and is not an adequate reference that should ever reflect on, or replace a thorough risk assessment. Again many so called security companies having no idea of how to provide good service will only concern themselves with guest/patron numbers, not the use of or geography of the location. The type of event, the layout of the building etc. The modern approach for many is to focus more on appearance rather than the ability to provide service. There should always be a minimum of two door staff at any location, no matter how small the venue. Yes security numbers should increase and reflect guest numbers but this should be decided by multiple factors not by a single principle. One Door Person can not maintain a safe environment. You cannot control access unless the door is covered, in the same respect you cannot monitor for disorder or unacceptable activity unless the public areas are patrolled.

Conditions of Entry

Security is employed to monitor and control access to the premises, in line with the companies admission policy and the Law.

- Maintain a safe environment
- Provide customer assistance
- Minimise risk
- Bag and person searches (with customer permission)
- Control access
- Patrol & monitor
- Team work

Observations & Visual Assessment

As in any security role rapid visual assessment of customers and the environment in which you are operating is vital to the success of your duties. Security is not purely reactionary, it is provided to pre-empt and if possible avoid conflict and danger. This is why those on the door and those in the venue must work in tandem, and to this end a keen eye for detail is required. Being able to monitor those you feel may be overly intoxicated and assess the body language of patrons is a sign of a security professional.

Assessing Aggression

Sometimes aggression is an obvious thing, when we think of it we often imagine aggressive actions. The physical or verbal element is often the final stage and if we are monitoring successfully we can sometimes intervene before a situation deteriorates.

Indicators

1) Facial expression – regardless of the words spoken your face will give away your intent,
   a) Clenching teeth / tightness of lips
   b) Reddening of the face
   c) Lack of blinking / extended eye contact

2) Stance – Stance may be staggered or weight constantly shifting
3) Exaggerated movement
4) **Fists clenched** (even when hands are by their side, **PRIORITY ASSESSMENT**)

Team Work

The old adage of being only as a strong as your weakest link is especially true in the security industry. It is often not about size, or the ability to look menacing, it is more about knowing your trade and being a good team player. Looking the part is one thing but stepping up when you are needed is totally different. You are there to help and that includes in the event of hostility. You need to be able to avoid issues happening but at the same time be able to deal with problems when and if they arise. If you are not prepared or confident enough to come to the aid of your colleagues then you are in the wrong job. In the same breath it must be mentioned that being over zealous is sometimes just as bad. Rushing into situations sometimes takes them to a level that you would prefer to avoid. It is a case of providing a service, supporting your team and reacting quickly and correctly, not creating the problems in the first place.

> *"Talent wins games,*
> *but teamwork and intelligence*
> *wins championships"*
>
> Michael Jordan

Request to Leave

As an agent working on behalf of a licensed premises you are perfectly within your rights to request that a patron leaves for reasons of unacceptable behaviour, disorder, criminality or safety. Some will leave willingly and politely, often they will voluntarily leave under protest. If you have decided that a patron is no longer welcome then their protests could be extremely verbally aggressive. This should not be taken personally, rather just a projection of their discomfort regarding not wishing to leave. Never be tempted to engage in argument with the person, this validates them, and as you have requested they vacate the premises their point has no validation. In some cases ejection from the premises will be required. This should never be undertaken by one door person, you have to consider the reason for removal and your safety and that of other patrons. The situation must be controlled and guidelines for restraint, if no other action is possible must be followed.

Remember the SAFER approach ?

Step back – Assess - Find Help – Evaluate – Respond

Crossing the line

Being aware of the threat is being in possession of as much information on a situation as possible. Assessing the dangers and events then using your best judgement combined with common sense and the training you have or should have received in order to facilitate the correct response.

You are employed by the venue, and it is that venue where you are providing your services and going off site is a judgement call. If you have removed a person who was a threat inside the building and their actions are the same outside are they still a threat? If they are at the door shouting in your face then they may be. If they are in the street shouting threats then probably not, moving into the street to interact with someone should only be done if you have justification to do so. Is there an immediate threat to life or injury and are your actions lawful?

You must continually reassess threat as situations change, restraining somebody for an action in one location may not be justifiable in another. This is not to say you should always stand and watch just because something is taking place off your site of operation. You have to use common sense and act within the law. You have a responsibility to your employer but you also have a duty as a citizen to act if the circumstances dictate.

Pub watch

Pub watch works in the same way as a shop watch scheme does. It allows for the sharing of intelligence between venues and the local authority in order to reduce offender rates. It not only allows patrons to be barred from one venue but all in the local area and this threat does a lot to deter. Also having such close connections between venues acts as an early warning for possible trouble and alerts staff to hazards and threats in the area. Working in conjunction with community CCTV control centres can add an additional eye in the sky when it comes to gathering evidence and summoning the emergency services if required.

Controlling Queues

All events; venues, concerts and public attractions have to implement measures in order to manage the influx of customers, and control and promote safety while they are accessing or moving around on site. As with all aspects of public safety staff undertaking this duty should obtain adequate practical crowd management and spectator safety training prior to deployment. As always prior planning and thorough risk assessment should be carried out. All events which attract the public will, in order to control influx, require queueing. All of which must be managed, and be seen to be managed by the public, especially if they are doing so for extended periods. Good customer service is required in this situation in order to instruct, advise and inform. Try to keep those waiting informed as much as possible, many complaints and resulting hostility comes from the lack of information, rather than the duration of the wait.

Implementation

Queues should be managed in accordance with promoting safety and practical application. The queue should not Impose on or restrict other pedestrian traffic or cause serious congestion to the activities of others. The management of the influx must reflect the numbers involved. If not enough personnel are tasked to deal, the situation can and will deteriorate and control will be lost. Barriers and cordons must be placed correctly and safely allowing for ease of use.

Type of cordon

- Filter Cordon – A line of security or marshalling staff which face the approaching crowd allowing them to be directed as security assessed as they filter inside.
- Barrier Cordon – A physical line of personnel in order to contain and direct.
- Safety barriers, to block or filter
- Notices to provide customer information regarding admission conditions
- Instructional signs or advisory personnel placed well in advance of queue to give clear instructional advice

CHAPTER FIFTEEN
Basic Terrorism Awareness

Unfortunately the risk of terrorism is a constant concern. Whether in the news headlines after an event or during a period of what may appear to be dormant activity, the concern and our response in order to reducing the risk remains the same. When we think of terrorism it is often easy to automatically think of the latest threat or the most recent attack. This will focus your mind in relation to an immediate threat but it should be remembered that an immediate threat is still only one in a list of current threats. Many may be dormant but they are still there and must always be considered. It is the duty of every person regardless of their job or position to remain vigilant and be socially aware, but in doing so still be able to go about their daily activities with the minimal of disruption. Those that operate in the security industry should possess a level of continued vigilance as part of their nature and approach to not only their work but also throughout their interactions whether in a paid role or not. It is a citizens duty to protect but it is also part of the trade craft of those qualified, experienced and knowledgeable to help by providing their expertise in risk assessment, observation and Immediate Action.

All employers have a duty of care to their staff and must put in place considerations and contingency planning in order to minimise the risk of terrorism. But this responsibility and duty of care is not solely down to them. It cannot work without you playing your part, whether you work for a large company, a lone worker or you are just a person walking to the shops, you have a responsibility as an individual to others.

Recognising Threat

We can all recognise the ultimate result of a threat often by the unfortunate manifestation of that threat into a disaster emergency situation. The question here is how do we recognise the threat in the first place. This is easier to do if we have information and communications in relation to a specific threat or risk but in the absence of this intelligence it is down to those on the ground with local knowledge of the environment observing and monitoring, paying attention to things which may appear out of place, items discarded, vehicles and persons who's activities may raise concern. For those employed in the security industry these tasks are your bread and butter and you should be observing, assessing and reporting any of these activities. If something doesn't feel or look right then trust your instincts and act on it, it is better to be wrong than be right but remain silent.

Intelligence Gathering

If you see or even feel something is not right, then if the situation permits report it if at all possible to your CCTV control room, they can then start recording video evidence and alert the authorities. Acts of terrorism take planning. You may be observing hostile reconnaissance therefore if something doesn't look right record as many details as possible. CCTV monitoring of a suspect allows for covert evidence of a persons activity; what they are doing, who they meet, where they go and locations that they give special attention to, and if possible can follow them to a vehicle recording the details which can be passed to the police. If you work in a uniformed role you may be approached and passed verbal intelligence. If that is the case take all threats seriously and treat them as such until proved otherwise. It is not the role of a private security officer to determine the validation of the information received, that is the responsibility of the police.

Vehicles

Vehicles should at all times be monitored if they enter a controlled area, any vehicle parked for extended periods without reason, or vehicles which are not expected or appear out of place should be investigated and concerns reported.

Cleaning and Waste

Security personnel should routinely as part of their patrols pay close attention to bins and waste facilities in public locations. It is much easier to secrete devices within or next to a bin without raising suspicion. For the same reason a good cleaning routine should be implemented. It is harder to notice things out of place if rubbish is allowed to build up. Therefore if you are working providing security at a venue it is advisable to report bins and locations which are getting overwhelmed, while at the same time inspecting them for any out of place or suspect items. It is also now standard operating procedure for many public buildings to use transparent waste bags. This allows for waste material to be inspected without being interfered with or moved in the bag. This is a logical pro-active approach to minimising risk, as avoiding having bins is often not practical and therefore using see through bags reduces the subsequent risk involved with having them.

Terrorism Risk Assessment

Risk assessment allows you to identify vulnerabilities and create an awareness of possible threats and the impacts they may create.

Ask yourself

- What is the current security climate like?
- Is there anything about the organisation, building or staff for which I provide service which may attract terrorist activity?

- Are we associated with high risk or high profile individuals or organisations which may be the target of terrorism?
- Could we suffer from, and how would we react to a local attack which is not directly at our location but would have a knock on effect?
- Could we suffer collateral damage by a nearby attack?
- Do we have anything that a terrorist may wish to use to further their aims? (materials, expertise, access to other premises etc.)

Confirm your assets

Decide what needs protecting and where your vulnerabilities lie.

- People (staff, members of the public, visitors)
- Physical assets (building and fabric)
- Data (information - electronic & paper)
- Operational procedures (essential critical services)

Public Footprint

What information is known publicly about the operation of the business, the directors and employees and the practices of the company and any individuals. Could this information attract a threat. If so limit the information you release to the internet, news outlets and customers, include all third party contract employees in this assessment and promote contractors to sign confidentiality agreements as loose lips really do sink ships. Raising your public profile must only be done if it does not increase risk.

Physical Security

Physical security can be seen, and if seen to be implemented professionally, goes a long way to countering the threat of terrorism. Regular uniformed patrols combined with electronic surveillance is often the first line of defence in relation to deterring and detecting activity.

Staff Training & Awareness

Security staff training should be a continuous exercise throughout your career. Studying and keeping up to date with current threats and counter-measures, and creating drills and training exercises in order that you can provide exceptional service. It is your duty to promote this ethos throughout the company and environment you operate in. Offer support to colleagues whether they are security workers or not. The task of providing security and minimising risk falls on the shoulders of every worker and you should be in a position to assist, offer support and advise.

Any procedure or countermeasure must hold up to scrutiny and therefore in order to assess its worthiness must be operationally rehearsed and tested. By doing so you can highlight things that work well and replace procedures which do not. Promote an atmosphere of free thinking discussion, as this is one of the best ways to highlight and focus attention on some of the staff concerns in relation to security training.

One particular benefit of offering a "free thinking all inclusive" staff approach to training, where every persons view is valid, often highlights shortfalls in the structured provided training provision offered by many outside agencies. They often fail to provide courses specific to the environment in which you are operating. By including all staff and combining that with the procedures and practices of the company you can implement a training package which is more easily absorbed by the staff in that particular environment, resulting in the training providing answers to the problems, not highlighting more questions and adding to staff confusion.

Bomb Threat

The majority of bomb threats are received by telephone. Thankfully most of which are hoaxes, called in by those with malicious intent. But some hoaxes are called by those who wish to terrorise, alarm and cause disruption. It must be remembered that all threats must be taken seriously and it is a crime to make a malicious bomb threat. No matter regarding the concern of validity, all reports must be passed to the police immediately.

Intention

1) To disrupt, divert attention or test response.

2) Threats or warning of a genuine device. In order to avoid casualties or divert blame of casualties being suffered. Even a genuine threat may provide disinformation or inaccurate intelligence.

Principles of Receiving a Telephone Threat

Consider your immediate action response to receiving a call of this nature.

1) Is it possible to record the call
2) How do I alert others while remaining calm and actively listening.

If you work for what may be deemed as at high risk of receiving bomb threats such as media corporations, government buildings, hospitals, hotels etc. all calls should automatically be directed to a telephone switchboard or a security hub. This filters and restricts the staff numbers that a threat may be relayed to.

When it comes to alerting others while remaining calm and not interrupting the caller or drawing attention from the caller it is advisable to, if working in a team, have a pre-determined hand signal that denotes threat. And by showing that signal instructs them to go silent and and carry out immediate action drills in relation to the threat. For example while you are concentrating on the detail of the call they can alert security control or designated individuals.

Again this is why security professionals always possess a pocket book. Details can be obtained and recorded immediately, as the situation may not wait for you to find a pen and paper.

The first key thing to remember is stay calm. A person is relaying important information and that is your immediate focus.

It is advisable to create a crib sheet of questions and actions in order to promote your immediate action response in relation to receiving a bomb threat.

I.A.D Immediate Action Drill

1) Switch on/activate recorder (if possible).
2) Identify your location to the caller.
3) Signal to others (threat call)
4) Record(Note) the exact wording of the threat.

Ask **(The 5 W 's)**

5) Where is the bomb right now?
6) What does it look like & what type of device?
7) When will it explode?   (Details add to validation)
8) What will cause it to explode?
9) Who placed the device?
10) Why?

Secondary Questions

Ask

12) What is your name & address
13) What is your telephone No.

It is difficult to imagine anyone actually releasing the information requested in the last two points but it is worth a try obtaining it. Also point 13 can be avoided if your business operates a caller display and the caller fails to withhold their number, so check that.

Record (Post Call)

1) Time and duration of call
2) Names of those you have informed
3) Time 999 contacted
4) Number at which call received
5) Sex of caller
6) Approx age
7) Nationality (Accent)
8) Language type spoken, e.g. Well spoken, irrational, reading from script
9) Background noises, e.g. aircraft, traffic, etc. which would indicate possible location.

There is a lot of information here, hence why creating a list and carrying it in your pocket book for reference is a good idea.   Remember the more we drill the more fluid situations become.

Creating a Security Plan

All premises require a security plan taking into account the practices and use of the building. The plan should be put in place by a designated security co-ordinator or manager. It is their duty to make all staff aware of procedures but it is also the duty of all personnel, especially those in the security sector to actively enquire and to understand all protocols in place and to highlight where they are lacking.

Emergency Communication Plan

All premises and teams require an emergency communication plan. However this is often dictated by size and use of the building and numbers of individuals affected. From all staff email alerts, conference calling, radio transmissions to all site Public Address systems and bull horns. In an emergency getting out information regarding what actions need to be taken is of time sensitive importance. The style and type of information relayed will be dependent on the urgency of the incident. In some cases an assertive Tactical Dynamic Control (TDC) initiative will need to be undertaken.

Searching Premises

All business's and locations should be routinely searched. The frequency of such a search should be considered in proportion to the perceived threat. Promoting a culture of security and maintaining a well preserved clean environment makes it easier to spot things which are out of place and promotes the ability to act upon activity which may be suspicious thus allowing for a more effective search regime.

Developing a search regime

Consider the following points;

1) Rationale (reason for the search)
2) Areas to be searched (public, private area/ stairwells, corridors, toilets, lifts, car parks etc.)
3) What are you intending to find
4) When to be completed (routinely and responsive to information/intelligence)
5) Responsibility & report. Who is responsible for each area. Confirm all clear and report back
6) Pair up for searching, reduces the risk of things being overlooked or missed
7) What is the IAD (immediate action drill) in regard to finding something suspicious
8) What training is required to make searching more effective
9) Who is in command, search teams require co-ordination

Implement rally and muster points in clear safe locations in order to update and deploy teams in a controlled manner. Make sure those conducting a search are fully aware and familiar with the layout and location in order to promote an effective search. Time delays or losing staff is not an effective approach. Divide the areas to be searched and deploy teams to cover the entire site.

Suspect Package

A suspect package can take many forms; from a jiffy bag, a cigarette packet, to a large box or bag. In fact anything which appears out of place or is unexpected could be considered a suspect package.

Suspect Mail

In relation to mail you are looking for anything which seems out of the ordinary,

Things which may raise concern;

- Excessive postage (in an attempt to limit postal staff contact the item may be over priced with stamps rather than weighed and franked with a label)
- Unfamiliar return address or none at all
- Protruding wires or strange odour
- Not specifically addressed
- Restrictive markings
- Rigid/Bulky
- Lop-sided/Uneven
- Excessively secured(taped)
- Leaking
- Discolouration/Sweating

Content which may cause concern

- Powders/Liquids
- Unidentifiable items
- Threatening written material

If you accidentally open a Suspicious Package;

- Leave the item where it is
- Do not handle or clean any spillages
- Wash hands and remove any clothing that has been contaminated
- Evacuate the area
- Close doors as you leave
- Dial 999
- Wait in a safe location for emergency responders

Mail Handling

Whether working for a large corporation or a small business, if you are considering the threat of a postal attack you should have a designated location where post is delivered to for inspection, collation and possible opening. You may have a dedicated Mail Room staffed with personnel which are fully trained and equipped to deal with postal incidents or it may just be an office or reception where mail is handled by one person within the company. Regardless of this any location used to open and control the mail entering a building should be secure. Ideally a room solid in construction without partition or panel walls and separated or isolated from any air conditioning system. The solid walls and lack of cycled air allow for containment in the event of a contaminant release.

Biological / Chemical

If you suspect that an opened item contains possible biological or chemical material you must act with cross contamination in mind. Alert management and initiate a controlled evacuation. Avoiding continued movement of the item, closing doors and windows, along with shutting down the ventilation and heating systems reduces dispersal rate and speed. Unlike an evacuation in relation to a conventional suspected IED, those that have been in close proximity to the suspected item should be evacuated to a secure safe location away from those who have not been exposed.

Suspect Item in Public Area

As a security officer you may be tasked to investigate an item which may have been placed in a public location. More often than not items reported are bags and luggage accidentally left behind, or the owner of which is in the local area, and often as you approach the item will make themselves aware. However all situations should be approached with caution, implement SAFER and assess your surroundings. If CCTV is available it should establish observations on the location of the item prior to your arrival and those responding should confirm this prior to approaching the item. If the item appears to be a bag or some form of luggage, or even a shopping bag or package which is conducive to the environment, for example a suitcase in a hotel lobby or a retail bag outside or within that particular store. Subtly and calmly make enquiries in the local area. If no one confirms ownership they may at least identify how long the item has been there. If the location has CCTV capability they should already be spinning the cameras back in order to confirm how long ago it was left and by who.

Suspected I.E.D (Improvised Explosive Device)

On discovering a Device;

Remember: The 5 C 's

- CONFIRM
- CLEAR
- CORDON
- CONTROL
- COMMUNICATION & CALL 999

Confirm

This should be the simplest principle but as we are talking about IED's the "I" standing for Improvised indicates that items can be in any form. Therefore it is often down to the experience, training and competence of the individual who initially identifies the item as a threat.

Clear

The area at risk must be cleared in a calm manner. Panic will create issues of control. Those in the danger area must be guided by clear instruction towards safe areas and muster points. These areas must be checked and all routes confirmed clear towards those locations taking into consideration possible secondary devices, building fabric and possible damage or injury risk should an explosion occur during evacuation.

Cordon

Once the area has been cleared a firm cordon must be established. As each area is evacuated and confirmed as clear by the security presence this cordon can be expanded until it reaches its desired size for safety in relation to the device or threat. The cordon must be non porous and Tactical Dynamic Control must be implemented in order to prevent incursion which may result in loss of life. In simple terms the cordon becomes the border of an area which must remain sterile with no unauthorised entry permitted. In order to facilitate this you may have to assert yourself tactically in order to forcefully prevent if necessary unauthorised entry and promote compliance.

Utilising hazard tape clearly defines the perimeter of the danger area and safe zone allowing for a firm cordon to be established by officers and is a clear warning to members of the public. The tape should be placed to extend the full length of any access zone or open area and laid out midway of average body height in order to optimise line of sight. It is often baffling how some will ignore, or claim they have not noticed a line of brightly coloured hazard tape stretched across an area. Additionally it is wise to keep the tape taught and it should go without saying that it should be wrapped around secure objects or solid building fabric at regular intervals in order to maintain its level and reliability.

Cordon Perimeter distances

The following is the recommended minimum cordon distance in relation to the type, size and style of suspect device.

ITEM	DISTANCE (METRES)
Small – Briefcase, shoe box, rucksack etc.	100
Medium – Large suitcases, wheelie bins, cars etc.	200
Large – vans, trucks etc.	400

Minimum transmission distance (radio & electronic communications)	15 metres

However if it is at all possible to avoid using electronic communications it is advisable to do so.

These guidelines must be considered in relation to building fabric and environment and should be extended if required. Always remember to consider the risk of a secondary device.

Control

No situation or operation will be successful unless controls are in place to facilitate that success. The fluidity and accuracies of that control stems from training and pre-planning, knowing your duties and roll in any event in order to provide your service without hesitation. Knowing and drilling your immediate action on a regular basis does not remove risk totally but it allows you and the team to rise to any presented challenge. The situation can only be controlled if Tactical Dynamics are put in place and those entrusted to act do so, combining that with the ability to follow instruction from those qualified to give them, but at the same time have the confidence to understand the gravity of what is at stake. The actions and duties of those involved must be professionally implemented in a timely manner. Control of the scene must be maintained and well communicated to the team throughout, as failing to provide a firm controlled site and cordon would be an unacceptable risk to life.

Communication & 999

A free flow of structured communication is vital both up and down the command chain. It is imperative that the entire team and police are fully informed, communication should be in a fluid, controlled format. Only clear vital information should be passed to the team or public in order to promote compliance, and done so in a manner which can be understood.

Evacuation Plan

You must plan and assess the feasibility of any evacuation procedure. This should be coordinated in relation to the threat received. Whether you are a member of staff at a venue or a contractor only employed for the day you should be made aware of procedures regarding emergency global evacuation of the premises. Those with intimate knowledge of the site should be in total control. If you are a new employee or contract security employed to bolster the staff for a particular event you should be advised and appraised as to your role or duties in the event of an emergency.

Reasons to Evacuate:

- A credible threat has been received at the premises
- A threat has been passed to you by Police
- Discovery of a suspicious item internally
- Discovery of a suspicious item, package or vehicle externally
- An incident in the local area which the Police have alerted you to

Regardless of the style or type of threat you should alert and inform the Police in regard to all actions undertaken. Deciding and controlling the route of any evacuation is always a difficult dilemma and there are many factors to consider all of which will be dependant on the location and type of threat. If the threat is in one location, then passing clear instruction and deploying a security cordon to usher people away from the danger zone, herding them towards the correct exit is wise as mass uncontrolled movement may inadvertently direct people towards further danger.

One rule to remember is to find out if the threat is internal or external and the precise location. Once this is known then the contingency can be put in place. For example if a suspect package or vehicle is discovered outside of the building it may be safer to remain internal. If that is the case safe zones such as solid walled locations away from moveable fabric, building furniture and windows should be established. If evacuation is required then directing individuals away from danger and out to the farthest point must be done quickly and calmly. Evacuation should always be initiated by the Security manager but it is down to the competence of the team to appraise the manager of the need to act. And also the competence of the manager to employ those whose judgement they trust fully. Any evacuation must be done as an immediate action exercise, confidently controlled and implemented with fluidity. Assessment must be made with the information to hand at that moment. It is not a time to hesitate or fluster.

Depending on the size of the venue or building. The location and the location of the threat, a evacuation may take the form of;

- Full global evacuation (outside of building)
- Evacuation of part of the building (if threat is small and confined)
- Full or partial internal evacuation (evacuation to safe zone inside building)
- Evacuation of all staff and personnel and public not needed for emergency duties

Evacuation Instructions

Instructions in relation to evacuation must be issued in a calm controlled manner. Clear instructions should be passed to visitors, guests and staff. A well trained immediate action response should go into effect.

Response Grab Bag

A response grab bag is a bag containing emergency response equipment. They are placed in secondary locations and are used if the main control area becomes compromised or inaccessible due to an incident.

A typical kit may contain;

- Map of premises
- Emergency contact number cards
- Stand alone communications device
- Batteries
- Torch
- Hazard tape
- Keys or key code accessible equipment
- Small medical kit

The above is purely an expansion of the security professionals concept of an operational grab bag but rather tailored to the emergency needs of a particular location and risk.

Securing Hazardous Material

This material by definition poses a danger to public health either as a product in its natural state or as a result of its use. It is the responsibility of not only the employer but also the employee to make sure these materials are kept and maintained safely and securely in line with all Health and Safety and COSH legislation.

Visit : www.hse.gov.uk/coshh

It is therefore necessary for those in the security department or on site security detail to understand the use of the premises. What type of materials are either stored, used or allowed on site. This promotes greater control of the substances held and allows you to add this information to your threat assessment analysis. You need to be aware of how accessible these products are. The risks to health and how well known is it that these items are stored or permitted on site. What is your immediate action response for dealing with this hazard and are these products something which may be appealing to criminals and terrorists.

Active Shooter

This is a term that is often avoided, especially by the companies which should really be considering the risk more than they actually do. Many privately owned commercial venues seem so fearful of the public associating their venue with the risk of an attack they fail to prepare adequately enough.

An Active Shooter incident as you would imagine is one involving a firearms incursion by a terrorist or terrorists in order to attack, maim and kill as many people as possible. Therefore if you work at a venue that is considered a public attraction, has limited or no public access restrictions then you must put in place some form of training which should include practical exercises for the staff involved. Showing your staff a home office video should be the start of, not the entirety of your training programme. A fingers crossed, heads down and hope for the best attitude that is prevalent in many places is not acceptable. The idea of saying it wont happen here is foolish and I'm sure it was said in Paris before they were attacked the first time. The threat is no longer a new one nor is it confined to overseas or distant lands.

The term active shooter first came into public awareness on November 26 2008 when gunmen carried out a devastating assault across Mumbai, killing 166 people. Since then the term has been used to refer to incidents in Nairobi, Kenya 2013 at the West Gate Mall and the 2011 Angus Breivik attack in Oslo. And more recently in Paris, when the offices of satirical magazine Charlie Hebdo were attacked on 7th January 2015 killing 12 people and again in Paris on Friday 13th November 2015 when gunman and suicide bombers attacked the Bataclan Theatre, a sports stadium, restaurants and bars in the heart of the city killing 130 people and injuring many more. However before this term had ever been coined by any news outlet the UK had already suffered from violent attacks similar in nature if not in scale. Incidents such as Hungerford in 1987 killing 14, Monkseaton 1989 killing 1 and injuring 14 others. The Dunblane Primary school massacre 1996, where a gunman opened fire killing 16 children and 1 teacher, also in Cumbria 2010 another 12 people were murdered. All of which were carried out by a lone gunmen.

According to the UK Security Services they have actively disrupted 34 large scale terror threats aimed at the UK population since the 7/7 London bombings as a result of proactive intelligence gathering, monitoring and infiltration of terrorist groups. However the threat of terror, including the risk of an active shooter incident, remains high. With the well publicised increase in police firearms officers and training practices for such eventualities, it must be remembered that if a group of individuals slips through the intelligence net the firearms officers deployed will be in a reactive response to an incident during its occurrence. With often the only alert at a location of an incident being the sound of gunshots ringing out as the carnage unfolds.

Taking into consideration the imminent risk posed and the geographical delay of the arrival of law enforcement professionals to the scene, it is wise that all business's and individuals take measures to minimise risk. As any responders will on arrival first have to make assessment of the situation before they consider hard entry. It is vitally important that plans and procedures are not only designed but drilled and implemented by all business's which consider themselves at heightened risk. These procedures should be put in place to deal with the immediacy of the threat, and cannot involve the police as they will not be on scene during the initial stages of activation. Creating plans which are two fold, the primary objective dealing with the risk to life and how you counter that and the secondary of gathering intelligence and relaying that to the police, liaising and supporting those officers on arrival at the scene.

Training

When it comes to training many may say that training for such events in the work place is impossible, as you cannot create an environment that would correctly mimic the real thing and therefore it would not represent how people would react nor how the aggressors would respond in a real world situation. This could be said for any training, if you undergo first aid training you are dealing with pretend casualties and situations. In business they have management exercises and team building programmes which they seem to love forcing on staff. They claim they have merit, so why is value added to taking office workers away from their desks to build a raft out of pallets but not for providing training which could save lives. Another excuse often used is that it will upset and focus the minds of the staff on a negative aspect of risk and the possibility of it happening, even using the excuse that the staff would not be able to deal with it. All of these reasons for not providing training have been used, and shockingly used in reference to the training packages given to security personnel! However is there any other consideration more important than preventing loss of life? We cannot remove the risk completely but training, as in all things, minimises it.

It must be remembered that the basics of training for this type of threat is already embedded or should be in any business premises, especially those which attract large numbers either as visitors or employees. You will have evacuation procedures already in place. It is impossible to eliminate the risk but by adapting the training you should already be doing, you will increase awareness and promote an immediate action response.

UK Home Office Guidelines (Active Shooter Incident)

On hearing gun shots !!! Stay Safe !!!!

RUN

- If there is a safe route, Run.
- Consider your route and risk.
- Insist others come with you but don't let them slow you down
- Move swiftly and quietly
- Leave belongings behind

HIDE

- If you can't run, Hide
- Find cover from attacker
- The best location will create a substantial barrier between you and the attacker
- Lock doors or barricade yourself
- Move back from doors
- Silence phones
- Remain still and quiet
- Wait for danger to pass

TELL

- If you are able to evacuate move as far away as possible
- Dial 999 from a safe location
- Give your location and postcode if possible
- Give as much detailed information as possible (numbers, direction of travel etc.)
- Stop others from entering if it is safe to do so

Your fist priority in any incident is your own personal safety. If your personal safety is at risk you cannot be affective in promoting the welfare of others. The RUN HIDE TELL principle is a sound one for the individual in a immediate threat to life scenario. However if you are working in security, people will be looking to you for help, instruction and guidance. Therefore the training and calibre of the individual will be tested.

The following includes additional considerations of those with a security mindset.

CONFIRM / CALL / RESPOND (C.C.R)

CONFIRM

Gathering rapid, accurate real time intelligence on the ground without putting yourself at greater risk in doing so should be a priority.

- Confirm its a firearms incident
- Report to CCTV control and arrange for CCTV observation
- Confirm numbers of gunmen
- Confirm types of weapons and proficiency
- Description, clothing and carrying
- Confirm location and direction of travel
- What are there methods of communications
- Numbers of known casualties & people in nearby locations
- Confirm contingency planning and evacuation in progress

CALL

- Relay details via 999 to emergency services
- Communicate on all formats instructions to public and staff
- Use preplanned emergency radio channels for security personnel in case standard channel has been compromised

RESPOND

- Implement global evacuation procedures
- Secure and lock-down CCTV control room to maintain its use and avoid compromising that location, evacuate non essential control staff.
- Maintain situation video continuity
- Appraise security staff of the location of danger
- Utilise PA systems to warn of the danger area and keep it clear
- Utilise security staff to push back, evacuated individuals by expanding the perimeter and taking Tactical Dynamic Control of the situation.

Imminent Loss of Life

This is often a consideration which is either overlooked or avoided. In regards to this we are not referring to taking yourself from a position of safety to one of danger in order to be a hero, this is a last resort situation. If you cannot escape or hide and you are cornered and believe you are in imminent danger of death, then you must attack as a form of defence. Attack with full force hold nothing back. We are not discussing techniques for disarming an attacker just highlighting that the situation may arise when you need to as a last resort attack in order to facilitate an escape. Remember if you can remove the barrel of a gun from pointing at you, then it removes its effectiveness as a firearm.

Police Response

When the police initially arrive it is likely they will immediately and rapidly carry out an assessment of the threat in order to formulate their response, mode, speed and location of entry. It is imperative that information regarding numbers of offenders, types of weapons, their location and possible numbers of hostages/unaccounted for individuals and details regarding building layout and access is passed to them. This information should be collated and made available by the on site security manager. The first on scene supervising police officer should also be given an in-house radio or other means of communication with the on-site control room and if safe to do so should be escorted to that location in order to obtain real time information on events as they unfold.

As soon as the police arrive they will take charge of the scene and it is the duty of any security personnel to assist and support their needs and requests. Armed police on entering the building will move swiftly through clearing and securing areas as they do. Their first priority is to save lives and neutralise the threat posed. They will do this by using shock and ore compliance tactics. Therefore they will be assertive and aggressive in their dealings with all individuals they come across as they have to make split second decisions as to whether each person is a threat or not. It is imperative that if you are hiding in the building you follow the instructions of those officers to the letter. They will be pointing firearms at you until the situation is under control and it is established you pose no threat.

Therefore

- Follow their instructions
- Do not make any sudden movements
- Keep your hands empty, put down any items slowly
- Keep your arms raised fingers spread apart

- Avoid shouting, screaming or talking
- Remain calm

You will probably be aggressively directed at gun point by the officers to exit the building. On exit you will be held in a secure area and possibly cuffed with plastic cuffs. At this point you are being detained in order to initially confirm you are not a threat and you can be identified. Once this is done you will be released and offered medical assistance if required.

Applying the SAFER approach to the C.C.R

S	STEP BACK	STAY SAFE
A	ASSESS	CONFIRM (CCR)
F	FIND HELP	CALL (CCR)
E	EVALUATE	CONTROL MEASURES (CCR)
R	RESPOND	IMMEDIATE ACTION (CCR)

Your Immediate Action SAFER assessment of every situation should be automatic and adapted to the severity and importance of the task. Don't over analyse emergency situations in their entirety. It makes no sense to be preoccupied on insignificant elements, especially in risk to life situations. Assess that which poses the greatest danger and deal with it. The continued reassessment throughout will allow you to pick up on the lesser elements at a more opportune moment.

CHAPTER SIXTEEN
Detention

Depending on the role you undertake and what is expected of you by your employer, you may have to detain people by restricting their liberty. In simple terms "prevent them from making off". As stated earlier in this book any restriction of liberty comes in the form of an arrest, and we are only permitted to do so if we have a strong belief or evidence that an indictable offence has been committed, and it is not practicable to wait for a responding police officer to make the arrest themselves. Many in the industry and this includes employers seem frightened of the term "Arrest" and will say "We do not arrest we detain". This shows a severe lack of foresight and understanding. To detain somebody by placing them under arrest is lawful. To detain somebody who is not under arrest, and by doing so stop them from leaving if they choose to, could be seen as false imprisonment. If you do not feel their detention warrants arrest then why are you restricting their liberty in the first place?

The following includes points of consideration for controlling a situation in relation to securing the suspect and evidence, and the welfare in regard to doing so. If you regularly operate in the security industry, especially in roles such as retail or in a venue based environment, it would be advisable that you review the Police and Criminal Evidence Act 1984 (P.A.C.E) in relation to the detention of suspects. We may not be the police but we must take into account not only continuity of evidence but also the welfare and human rights of the individual.

www.legislation.gov.uk/ukpga/1984/60/part/IV

Compliant Customer

I have added this in order to point out, especially in retail or hospitality situations that we must always implement common sense and understand compliance. The common sense comes from assessing the gravity of the alleged offence and attitude of the person or persons you are dealing with. Taking into account all the information presented and the action or manner of the person you are interacting with, arrest may not be warranted and the customer may be unaware of any issue and in that case could be fully compliant. This is your judgement call. Providing you take responsibility, and monitor and reassess the situation as you go, you can always inform them they are under arrest should new information come to light or the situation changes. Compliance is always the best option if it is available to you.

Approach

Your physical approach to the suspect must always be risk assessed. You must take into account the benefits of approaching the suspect by entering their view in order not to startle or scare them, and by making them aware of you reduces the initial emotional impact or shock of being approached and embarrassed by the interaction. However if there is a strong risk of the suspect making off or destroying evidence then a hard stop may be required. It is your job to assess and react and be able to justify why you reacted in the manner you did.

Point of Arrest

Confirm Actions:

1) Identify yourself to the suspect

2) Inform them they are under arrest and the reason for the arrest

3) Caution them as soon as it is practicable to do so

Caution

"You do not have to say anything but it may harm your defence if you fail to mention something you later rely on in court, anything you do say may be given in evidence"

4) Escort them to a safe/controlled location

Securing Evidence

Items from the scene should be secured as soon as possible, this does not include items on the suspects person as searching the suspect is not permitted. Any items discarded by the offender must be recovered and recorded. Any witness testimony and/or CCTV evidence must also be safely recorded and made available to the police.

Three Person Detention Detail

When securing a suspect you must take into consideration the safety of those involved. This includes officers at the scene, the public, as well as the alleged offender. Guidelines are in place which advise the use of three persons to one offender. This allows the situation to be more easily and safely controlled.

Restraining

In some cases a suspect will be required to be restrained in order to protect not only themselves but also the public. Responding officers should, in a situation which may require physical intervention, know at what time and when to implement a physical hands on approach in order to take control of the situation and the suspect. Additional training and awareness of this key duty should be undertaken both of the law in relation to this action, and the physical intervention practical training element, with emphasis on positional asphyxiation. Combining this training with an understanding of how and when to implement it builds confidence in its practical application. It must be remembered that being confident, qualified and willing to in exceptional circumstances restrain an aggressor or absconder is one of the key roles of a security professional. This cannot be avoided if you are employed to apprehend offenders and maintain the safety of the public. A person who is unwilling to carry out this action, or hesitant due to a lack of confidence puts the safety of themselves and their colleagues at risk. It may seem like rather a daunting consideration, that is a natural state of mind. You are carrying out an action which is out of the ordinary, the uncomfortable unease which you may feel will keep you alert and keep complacency at bay. You need to be switched on, you never know what a person may have in their possession. Just as problematic are those officers which are often over zealous in these situations, physical restraint should only be used when warranted and justifiable. You not only need the confidence to act, but the common sense to show emotional restraint. The guidelines which cover this, as with all things are guidelines to promote welfare. Please do not confuse these things with your right to self defence.

Police

Immediately at the point of detention the police should be informed as any delay increases the duration the suspect is in your care.

Detention Room

Any business located within an environment where arrest or customer compliance issues are involved needs to designate an area where those which are required to remain can wait for the police. This area must be sterile and designed for the purposes of control. Chairs and office furniture should be kept to a minimum. Many establishments do not do this and will provide a make shift holding area should someone be arrested on site. In many cases this being the managers office. This may work if the detainee is compliant throughout, however if they are not or the situation becomes aggressive items in the room could be used to cause harm or injury either to themselves or others.

Holding room

- Should be clear of any foreign objects (unnecessary items/belongings)
- CCTV monitored (throughout, no breaks in continuity)
- Inspected prior to detainee arrival
- 3 officers should remain with suspect throughout
- Holding room searched immediately after detainee is removed

Concern for Welfare

You have to monitor and assess the welfare of those in your care throughout the duration they are being held. Any injuries either sustained at the point of arrest or otherwise must be recorded. And all provisions possible be available to maintain the continued welfare of the suspect.

First Aid / Medical

Medical treatment must be offered for any conditions suffered from, either received as a result of their detention or in relation to any pre-existing condition. Emergency medical provision made available where necessary.

Recording Information

All information relating to the incident, your actions, the actions of the alleged offender, statements of witness's and evidence must be recorded. This includes the CCTV of the holding area and of the event if available and released to the police to promote a prompt investigation of the alleged offence. In relation to the offender it is permitted for the arresting security officer to request the offenders details but not demand them. The alleged offender is also within their rights to refuse to give them. If that is the case the officer should record their refusal. Any details offered are to be recorded, and again passed to the police. It is not permitted for the arresting security officer to interview the alleged suspect in relation to the offence. This should only be carried out by the police officers in attendance. However any details in relation to the incident freely offered by the suspect should also be added to your police submission.

Searching Detainees

If you remember from earlier, a private security officer is the same as any citizen and has **no powers to search a person**, accept with their consent, which should only be in relation to condition of entry and compliance, never in any form of arrest or detention situation. In relation to arrest procedure only concentrate on the highlighted section of that phrase. The reason being it can have a serious detrimental affect on the continuity of the investigation and can risk the entire prosecution. If the offender draws items from their clothes or baggage, allow them to do so and record that they freely did, ideally this will be done in full view of recording CCTV cameras. By you, as the responding security officer, searching the suspect you not only risk injury from concealed items held in their belongings, you risk the evidence itself as they may accuse you of planting it. Therefore the only lawful search of the suspect and their belongings can and must be done by the police when they arrive. Understanding this point, that you cannot search the suspect but you are able to request (a request that they can either accept or decline) them to empty their pockets or bags, remembering this must be done on camera. You can never be sure what the suspect does or does not have in their possession, therefore always monitor their hand movements and do not permit them to reach into their pockets unless they are doing so under your instruction and while you are stood clear.

Wash Room Facilities

Any person under arrest has the right to use the facilities and basic provision must be made in order to allow them to do so. This is a basic human right, not to mention declining them may result in you having to clean up a mess. Considerations for the use of, and location, accessibility and practicality of the toilet facilitates must be made. The suspect who is in your care must be monitored, both physically by officers of the same sex throughout and if possible by CCTV while in transit to and from. The route to and from the facilities must be made sterile as well as the toilets themselves. By removing items from access corridors and securing the toilet facilities allows you to control the environment, promoting safety for not only your team but also the person in your care when doing so and in order to preserve continuity of the investigation, and not jeopardise it. A toilet and cubicle must be inspected and confirmed free of foreign objects prior to them being used, and again inspected and anything found recorded after the suspect has left the facilities. It is often the case, especially with you lacking the power to search the individual, they will attempt to discard any incriminating items as soon as it is conveniently possible and by failing to monitor you increase the risk of their success.

CASE STUDIES

PUTTING THE THEORY INTO PRACTICE

Up to now we have been considering the theoretical aspect and hopefully the thought provocation which has ensued. We are now going to put this theory into practice by reviewing a selection of case studies taken from real life security incidents, all of which took place within the retail and leisure venue environment. The location, due to its size, popularity and varied facilities spread over a large area makes it an ideal source of information for operational assessment.

Every case study in this section has been laid out firstly displaying a synopsis or overview of the details of the event in question. The second section will contain the actions of the individuals involved in the incident as they took place in real time with the information which was at hand. The final part on each case study will contain a post incident review in the form of a de-brief, where details of the actions involved are scrutinised away from the event in order to establish the particular areas which went well, and those considerations which may require procedural reassessment and improvement in order to avoid the repeat of an unfavourable action in the future.

A case study reflects true events and therefore will rarely demonstrate perfection. It will however highlight points for consideration and discussion. It is hoped that by careful review the reader will begin to understand the value of continually assessing their approach in order to maintain and raise standards. It should also promote in your own mind questions both in relation to the incidents listed and those you come across in your own lives.

Case Study 1

AGGRESSIVE INDIVIDUAL

Synopsis: Reports via control of an aggressive customer on premises at a store within a complex. Radio request for attendance no further details received.

Action:

Security officer one (SO1) responded to premises. (SO1) requested confirmation that complex CCTV cameras covered store front and entrance. The officer en-route also requested and confirmed that a second officer (SO2) was en-route and confirmed was in place with clear line of sight on (SO1) prior to entering. SO1 entered shop unit visually scanning throughout. SO1 liaised with staff who confirmed suspect had left the premises. No crimes reported by store manager. Description and direction of travel passed to control room. Unit staff advised no further action (NFA) and stood down.

De-brief:

SO1 responding knew that the centre complex CCTV was not connected to the store. Nor did it have the range to cover activity inside. Therefore he confirmed that the exit was under CCTV observation and he had a back up officer in place before he entered. This minimised risk to SO1, and provided rapid response and observational assistance from SO2 with eyes on. This should be standard operating procedure when entering a situation blind. The control room could not see and therefore any hostile event would go unnoticed, especially if SO1 had been attacked and unable to request assistance via his radio. It is always advisable for a minimum of two officers to attend an incident as a matter of safety. In this case the first responder felt it unnecessary for the second officer to enter with him, rather placing SO2 in an observational and responsive position outside. This may have been standard operating procedure for SO1 but sadly the complex security control group promoted a one officer no support approach. The first responder (SO1) overrode the complex SOP and rightly took responsibility for his actions and response.

Case Study 2

AGGRESSIVE INDIVIDUAL (2)

Synopsis: Reports via control of an aggressive customer on premises at a store within a complex. Radio request for attendance no further details received.

Action:

Security officer one (SO1) confirmed responding. Two further officers (SO2 and SO3) confirm via radio they are attending in a support role. SO1, not waiting for support attendance, entered the store and approached the staff. SO2 and SO3 arrive on scene and take up positions external to the shop unit one either side and out of site. Three to five minutes lapse no radio communication or updates given to support staff or control room. Four additional officers attend and position themselves again either side of the shop front. SO1 then exits confirming situation had calmed and security attendance was not needed. No further action (NFA).

De-brief:

SO1 responding entered shop without confirmation of CCTV coverage of entrance (remember no coverage inside unit). SO2/SO3 had confirmed as back up but neither entered the store nor do they position themselves with line of sight on SO1. Therefore they were not in optimum position to assist. Neither were the further two responders (X) who also took up position without line of sight. Updates from SO1 were slow and there was no CCTV support. Radio's do not always work especially in dense environments or areas with interference. SO1 could have been getting bounced around like a pea in a whistle with the six officers outside being none the wiser. If only one had changed position allowing for a clear line of sight into the shop unit that officer could have monitored the welfare of the colleague inside.

Case Study 3

DOMESTIC ALTERCATION

Synopsis: Intelligence led report received via concerned member of public and passed to CCTV control room. Information was in relation to an aggressive verbal altercation between a male and female in the car park. Radio requests for officers to attend location.

Action:

Two officers confirmed attendance and make their way to the car park. On arrival SO1/SO2 see a male and female believed to be in their early twenties extremely intoxicated. SO1 approaches and separates both parties. SO1 then speaks to the male, while SO2 stands with his back to the male leaving the female to stand off by herself. SO1, after obtaining the gentleman's version of events then speaks to the female. Both had calmed and no crimes reported. The couple admitted they were heavy in drink as they were celebrating the female's 18th birthday. They were both advised regarding their conduct and they stated they were heading home as the males mother was on her way to collect them. SO1 updated the control room and requested they monitor the couple while on site. The couple were remotely monitored as they made their way to the rear of the car park. They were then seen on camera to get into a vehicle (vehicle details recorded). The intoxicated male getting into the drivers seat. CCTV control then 999'd the incident to the police as the vehicle moved off at speed. CCTV maintained continuity as the vehicle sped off the car park onto the carriageway (still on site). The vehicle on arriving at a roundabout (RA) did not slow down. Taking the RA at speed, did one full circuit of the RA lost control coming off the road and crashing coming to rest embedded in a lamp post. All available officers were then requested to attend the scene. SO1/SO2 from the initial incident responded along with two further officers, one of which was in an emergency response vehicle. The occupants from the offenders vehicle were fully conscious and breathing, had no visible injuries and declined first aid. They were escorted from the vehicle and seated on the grass embankment away from the highway. The offenders vehicle was then secured and traffic management implemented. The police, who were already en-route, were swiftly on the scene and the driver subsequently arrested on suspicion of excess alcohol. Traffic management remained in place until the vehicle was recovered and the area cleared.

De-brief:

On arrival at the initial incident the parties were correctly separated. This minimised the risk of conflict but as SO1 was talking to the male SO2 should have, while maintaining line of sight, spoken to the female. Instead SO2 stood with his back to the incident, if his intention was to remain with the first officer for safety reasons his positioning removed his usefulness, which meant he was not assisting and not able to prevent or react to an assault if needed. The initial situation was calmed but by maintaining CCTV in a concern for welfare role the situation could be monitored and continuity of evidence established in relation to the second incident.

Case Study 4

VEHICLE COLLISION (HIT AND RUN)

Synopsis: Member of security staff witness's a two vehicle (RTC) whilst stood down on a welfare break.

Action:

A Security Officer witness's vehicle (1) reverse from a parking space at speed ramming into another vehicle (2), which was parked in a designated bay on the other side of the car park it then proceeded to make off. The security officer radios a priority message to control requesting them to take up observations of the vehicle (1) driving recklessly off site. The security officer records details of both vehicles involved in the incident, including damage and paint transfer details and draws a sketch diagram of the incident in his pocket book demonstrating start position and direction of travel. Vehicle (2s) registered keeper and local police informed.

De-brief:

This is a case of being in the right place at the right time. If the officer was not on the scene the incident probably would have gone unreported and the owner of the damaged vehicle would have had no redress. The swift actions of the security officer meant offender details were secured, although a description of the driver could not be obtained due to the speed with which events unfolded. It is always wise to attempt to record a description of the driver in case they refute their presence, as it helps to link them with the scene and when added to your statement aids the success of the prosecution. The quick alert to the CCTV control room allowed them to obtain valuable footage, not of the actual vehicle contact but evidence of their aggressive driving. It also reinforces your details just in case you missed anything in regard to colour of vehicle, make and model. This is another reminder as to why even on break a professional always keeps their radio with them and switched on.

Case Study 5

PLAIN CLOTHES SURVEILLANCE

Synopsis: Retail Complex CCTV Control room request plain clothes surveillance assistance to monitor a suspicious male on site.

Action:

Two plain clothes surveillance officers are tasked to take up eyeball on a target in order to monitor the suspects movements as they travel from store to store making purchases. Updating each other and their control centre as they do in order to facilitate a smooth investigation. The target enters each store and so do the surveillance officers, maintaining line of sight throughout. The surveillance continues for approximately one hour and no crimes or suspicious activity are detected. The team stands down. However shortly thereafter the target male makes a report to a member of staff at the complex that two people were continually following him. And in doing so relayed some of the conversation he overhead from the surveillance team while they were on the phone to each other passing intelligence.

De-brief:

This incident demonstrates poor drills and training. The report which the complaining customer submitted confirmed the continuity of events. The terminology and language the target suspect claimed he overheard combined with the review of the CCTV went a long way in substantiating his version of events. Surveillance is permitted especially as a tool and means of gathering evidence of activity. But it becomes an invasion of privacy and a human rights violation if the target of your surveillance becomes aware, and if continued could be considered harassment. It also becomes a time wasting exercise if the target is alerted to your actions. With them being aware, it would alter how the suspect acts, with them now being highly unlikely to commit a crime. Therefore as a surveillance officer not being pinged (seen) should be the top priority. Any team, regardless of size, should rotate in order to minimise the risk and pull officers out if they suspect that is the case, and if necessary pull back or stand down altogether if practicable. If CCTV is available as a tool use it. Good communication with differing CCTV environments and services will facilitate that. Also being so close that the subject can overhear operational details, even if you accidentally cross the subjects path or while within their vision is ridiculous.

Case Study 6

MEDICAL - ROAD TRAFFIC COLLISION (RTC)

Synopsis: Reports received of a two vehicle RTC. Motorcycle collided with car and motorcyclist knocked off bike and lay in highway with members of the public in attendance.

Action:

CCTV Control Room alert staff on site to a RTC at a busy junction roundabout. While monitoring the incident remotely, response is not ordered by control as the incident has occurred off site on the public highway. The location of the accident off site is 30 metres from the main gate to the complex grounds. Medically trained Security personnel in close proximity request permission to attend. Response via the radio net replies " We cannot instruct staff to deploy as it is off site and not insurance covered". CCTV in the mean time have reported the incident to the police and ambulance service. A few officers repeat their request to attend and CCTV control repeats their previous response. Two nearby security personnel take up observational positions at the perimeter of the site and they are joined by the on site emergency response vehicle. Reports are now passed of there being two off duty nurses in attendance at the scene however this is unconfirmed as verbal confirmation has not been received nor contact made with those at the scene of the incident. Ambulance arrives shortly after and the paramedics remove the casualty to hospital.

De-brief:

Remember the wording of the control room response " We cannot INSTRUCT staff to deploy as it is off site and not insurance covered". Yes it was off site and yes it was on the busy public highway, but by saying the word "instruct" you could consider they were just removing the responsibility for your safety away from the company and placing it in the hands of the individual. It therefore becomes an issue of conscience as to whether a person on seeing someone injured can really stand by, especially when they have the training to be able to assist. Yes it was unfolding on the public highway, but you minimise risk by additional responders donning High Visibility clothing and implementing traffic management, an acceptable response considering the risk of lose of life. The officers which were 30 metres away had access to life saving equipment. And the response vehicle which had come from one side of the building only to pull up at the edge of the working site was fully kitted with medical supplies and emergency lighting. Luckily the paramedics and police were swiftly on scene, but questions should be asked as to why those who could have assisted refused to take responsibility for their own actions and pro actively preserve life. The bigger question however is..... how would you react in the same situation?

Case Study 7

FIRE ALARM ACTIVATION

Synopsis: Integrated control room fire alarm panel activates (during business hours - public in building). Location identified all available officers deployed to establish cause.

Action:

Control Room transmits "All call signs Echo Foxtrot, Echo Foxtrot (emergency Fire code). All available call signs respond to....... (location)." Responding call signs then transmit acknowledgement and confirm en-route. Fire alarm activations by their nature are time sensitive and rapid response to such an incident is carried out by all officers on hearing the Fire code. Six security officers are confirmed as responding. SO1 and SO2 are the first two officers on scene, the location being a large clothing retailer located within a much larger leisure complex. Immediate assessment by the first two officers as they approach the premises and enter shows no initial visible signs of smoke or fire.

The store looks as though it has been evacuated. The two responders make their way to the rear of the department store in search of retail management, assessing for dangers as they progress. SO1/2 discover the door to the staff area and offices at the rear of the shop is secured. Therefore they are unable to gain access to the managers office or to the alarm panel located within. The alarm panel within the store is the only means of confirming the location of the actual activation within the shop in order to allow for physical inspection. Radio communication with the control room cannot be established due to poor signal and interference from building fabric. Therefore SO1 and 2 make their way back to the front of the department store in order to exit and re-establish communications with the control room in order to update them. On the way they meet up with another four security officers. All six officers now make their way at speed in order to safely exit the store. On approaching the exits the officers discover that the fire shutters had activated throughout the shop unit. The purpose of these is to reduce the risk of a fire spreading within the store unit but also from spreading to other buildings therefore shutters were also on the front public entrances, thus hampering and now blocking the escape route for the officers in attendance. The six officers now being trapped inside unable to establish communications and this remained the case until the alert had ended and the shutters re-set.

De-brief:

As you can imagine this incident did not go well, and highlighted a lack of operational training and experience. Thankfully the activation was a false alarm. Had it been a real fire loss of life would have been a distinct possibility. The store manager had in fact made contact with the control room by phone. Unfortunately however this was not in time for any information to be relayed to the responders before they entered and subsequently lost communication ability. If during a fire activation a member of store staff was given the pre-planned role of emergency liaison as part of their Standard Operating Procedure

(SOP), who would then during a fire or emergency situation exit the store safely and meet first responders in a designated location in order to advise and update officers before they enter. This would make a great deal of sense as those that work in that location have a greater understanding of the layout and should have been aware of the fire shutter system. Thus eliminating the need to enter an environment blindly. During this incident the lack of working communication and preventative intelligence put the security staff at great risk, rectifying the issue of poor communications is a serious health and safety concern. There is a great deal which could have been learnt from this failed incident and many things put right. However concerns raised at the time have never been acted upon and the same risk still remains. When that happens you run the risk of history repeating itself and the end result next time not being so lucky.

Case Study 8

FIRE ALARM ACTIVATION (2)

Synopsis: Integrated control room fire alarm panel activates (out of hours no public in building). Location identified (department store) all available officers deployed to establish cause.

Action:

Control room transmits emergency fire response code (e.g. Echo Foxtrot) to respond to fire alarm activation at location (X). All call signs confirm receipt of transmission and that they are en-route. The activation occurred out of hours and as a result there are no members of the public in the building and the store front shutters are already lowered for that reason. Responding officers make their way to the stores security office located at the rear and accessible by way of the car park. Four officers are now in attendance and on arrival the access door is locked which would be expected, the officers had to bang on the door repeatedly to get the attention of the store night security guards stationed inside. Eventually after approximately 2 minutes the door is opened and the four complex security officers enter. As the officers enter the premises one immediately asks the stores security **"what is the cause of activation"**? This is met by a confused look from the store staff as they respond "**we don't know.**" The officers then ask where is the fire alarm panel. They are then directed to an office with the panel bleeping and flashing on the wall. Looking at the screen on the panel it reads FIRE zone 4.

On reading this and thankfully having working communications this information was relayed to the complexes control room. At this point they turned to the on site security to ask them to confirm the location of zone 4. They were unable to answer this enquiry positively as they did not know the zone locations relating to the panel. The first responders then ask **"have you carried out a sweep of the building."** The in store staff answer yes, however the response and wording lacked any confidence meaning the responders struggled to believe that to be true. The four responding complex officers then sweep the building from top to bottom. Splitting into two teams each taking a member of in store staff with them to guide them around the departments and levels. However it is quickly realised that the in-store officers are neither familiar with the layout nor fire procedures. The alarm call is then passed to the fire service and appliance response becomes automatic. The complex officers continue their sweep with the fire service now en-route. Automatic fire prevention shutters are now activated on the front of the store in order to protect against any spread of smoke/fire and to keep it contained.

The CCTV control room keeping up remote observations of the store in order to relay any visual indicators of fire or emergency to the officers on the ground whilst keeping observations for approaching fire appliances in order that they can be met and updated as soon as they arrive. The building is swiftly and methodically checked for signs of fire or persons within. All the officers then return to the ground floor area rear entrance and meet up with and appraise the attending fire service. The fire service on arrival are shown the panel and told of the lack of usable intelligence in relation to the incident. The Fire Brigade being on site take control of the incident and utilising the complex security officers carry out a second search and inspection of the building. On completion the ranking fire officer confirms that he is happy that there is no fire or threat and it is OK to stand down. The panel in the store is re-set first and does not go off again indicating that the system is working. This information is passed to the control room belonging to the complex and their system is then re-set also.

De-brief:

On arrival the complex security officers were not met by any staff from within the shop unit and there was a delay due to the doors being locked before they could enter. On entering there was no confident response to questions asked, nor was there any relay of information from the staff who were employed to secure the store overnight. The store staff could not confidently inform in a manner that was believable that they had carried out a search of the premises. They had no understanding of the fire alarm panel, how it worked or the zones in which the system related to nor of any fire precautions for the store in which they worked. Therefore they were not in any position to professionally assist during any fire emergency. Any member of security employed in a building as a base of operations and to provide service to that privately owned and managed premises must understand the layout of the building and the workings and procedures of the fire alarm system and how the panel relates to the zones within. This should be standard basic induction training when you start working in a location, especially when you are employed to provide that form of service. The department store referenced was employing contract security personnel from an outside provider. This can mean that communication between companies may be difficult. It may also mean that the people paying for a service are being short changed by not actually getting the service they need. However you can blame poor communication as to the reason some things are overlooked but not when it comes to what should be standard operating procedure for the individual officers themselves. It is the responsibility of the individual operator to risk assess the environment in which they work and understand the duties required. Being a professional means actively understanding the elements needed to keep yourself and others safe. By considering the risk element these officers would have known that being fully aware of layout, procedure, zones and alarm panel was part of their job and by not pro-actively minimising risk they put themselves and others in increased danger.

Case Study 9

CHEMICAL CYLINDER (BLOW TORCH) FIRE

Synopsis: Site control room receive a radio transmission from a member of cleaning staff that there is a fire in the public dinning area of the complex. Camera observations are taken up and emergency coded response transmitted to all security personnel to respond to that location.

Action:

Control room transmits emergency fire code (Echo Foxtrot) and requests available call signs to respond. Location passed by staff member and CCTV observations are taken up to update the responding officers as to the nature of the event. A call sign en-route confirms his attendance as the control room transmits a situation update informing the first responder that they have located the incident and that it is in fact a small hand held style gas cylinder stood upright, fully engulfed in flames in the middle of the public dining area. Members of the public and designated area cleaners are in close proximity to the incident. The cylinder continues to burn with flames now rising 2-3 foot from above the valve, with flammable liquid pouring down and away from the cylinder. At this time cleaning staff and public are still within 5 metres of the fire watching on as the first responder arrives on scene. Securing a CO2 extinguisher the security officer approaches, tackles and extinguishes the device as staff and the public look on. The situation was controlled eventually. The threat dealt with and the item was confirmed safe and removed to a secure location.

De-brief:

This is an interesting case as it allows for the assessment of an Immediate Action response to a threat in a real world, real time situation. The first responder in securing a fire extinguisher and immediately dealing with the most important element namely the fire itself assessed the level of threat and dealt with it accordingly. However the other staff on scene namely the cleaning staff should have logically known to clear the area. This did not happen nor did further responding security personnel actually get involved with the incident. The cylinder was made safe, cooled and removed to a secure location by the first responder. Further staff should have responded and on seeing the fire being tackled should have prioritised clearing the danger area of the public. Unfortunately bystander apathy took effect;

Definition -

"The bystander effect, or bystander apathy, is a social psychological phenomenon that refers to cases in which individuals do not offer any means of help to a victim when other people are present. The probability of help is inversely related to the number of bystanders." This apathy also relates to incident response, assuming others have it covered and not comprehending the risks and dangers involved.

The video of this incident was later used as part of an in-house Fire Marshal training course. The CCTV footage showed complete continuity of the event but it also highlighted the lack of action on the part of other personnel. You can argue that the cleaning staff did not know what to do in the event of an emergency and highlight additional training for all staff. It does also highlight the importance that security and safety is the responsibility of all who work within the company, not just those in security. This site does correctly instruct other departments that during an emergency they should follow instructions given to them by security staff and assist in any way required. The main problem therefore was the lack of response and action from additional security support. No cordon and no push back of public was implemented. This reinforces the point that in situations which demand, you must understand and be able to carry out an Immediate Action response to threat. The CCTV footage clearly showed prior to first responder arrival that the only staff member at the scene did little more than pull a couple of chairs away from the cylinder by about 2 metres and you could see a young gentlemen who remained seated within 5 metres still munching on a burger. This highlights a concern regarding those companies which push their version of Customer Service training down the throats of the staff. It is right that you offer excellence in service but this does not begin and end with just a smile or by saying a generic "how can I help you?" without possessing the actual ability to assist. Surely the first priority in customer service is the preservation of life. This incident called for a rapid response and for assertive Tactical Dynamic Control to be implemented. This did not take place and escalation was only avoided by the quick thinking of the initial responder. But the bigger issue was the fact he had no support to assist him if the situation had deteriorated or changed.

The interesting aspect of the training review of this material raised a key point. The instructing fire officer on the course was asked how far back should the area be cleared. He responded with 20 metres which seems a concern. Is it not a gas cylinder full of pressurised flammable liquid? The cylinder was engulfed in flames top to bottom with a jet of fire shooting from the top. Whether the likelihood of it exploding due to the temperature (which could not have been ascertained) was high or low, it should still be considered as an explosive and bomb protocols implemented. Therefore 100 metres is considered the danger zone. If the item had exploded the risk of shrapnel would certainly extend past 20 metres. Another interesting point came from the people watching and reviewing the footage during this training course. They seemed more concerned with finding fault with the actions of the responder rather than the inaction of others. Which may highlight a concern that some may feel it is better not to act in some circumstances for fear of making a mistake. If that is the case for the individual it could be suggested that those people gain the confidence and skills to act or seek differing employment.

Case Study 10

SUSPICIOUS PACKAGE

Synopsis: Security Officer finds an unattended rucksack/back pack in a public area.

Action:

A security officer (SO1) on patrol comes across an unattended bag. The officer approaches the bag, picks it off the ground then radios the security control centre to inform them of his find and that he is en-route to their location with the item for safe keeping. The control centre refuses this action without further details. The initial officer then becomes confused as to why his request has been declined and a further officer is despatched to his location. On arrival the second officer (SO2) witness's the officer with the bag swinging it in a circular motion over his head. When asked why he was carrying out this course of action the officer had no response. But when he was informed that as he had not inspected it there was a risk their could be a unknown explosive or other dangerous items inside the officer responded with **"if it was a bomb it would have gone off by now."** The second officer inspected the item, confirmed it was no threat and took it to the controlled area.

De-brief:

The initial officer had in no way made any attempt to establish ownership of the bag nor had he considered what it may have contained. The control centre was correct with the limited information to refuse acceptance of the item. The officer first on scene approached the bag without making any assessment, without asking for CCTV support or advising anyone else of the situation. This officer did not implement SAFER in any fashion. He proceeded to, without making any visual inspection, lift the bag off the floor and begin waving it around in one hand while operating the radio with the other. The priority in this situation is assessing for your own safety and the safety of others. Visual inspection without disturbing the item is of utmost importance.

Case Study 11

ALLEGED THEFT

Synopsis: Reports received by control room of an alleged incident of theft occurring in an on site arcade and entertainment venue. Officers requested to attend in order to investigate.

Actions:

The on site control centre received a telephone call from one of the retail units within the site alerting them to an alleged theft that has occurred within their premises. Site security patrol officers are then deployed to that location to ascertain what has actually taken place. The officers en-route confirm attendance and request that control and other officers standby as radio communication will not be possible due to coverage once the officers enter the premises. The officers confirm the site CCTV control room have eyes on the front of the venue and make their way inside to the venue managers office. On arrival they speak to the manager who confirms that they have detained an individual on suspicion of theft. The officers then speak to and obtain details from the alleged victim, confirming her account and a description of the goods stolen; namely a white hand bag. The aggrieved person stated that she did not witness the actual theft but rather saw the alleged perpetrator brush against her at the time the bag went missing. At the point the bag was removed she claimed it was placed on the floor and not physically in her possession. The officers reassured and calmed the alleged victim, while one remained with her in a supportive role the other made his way to the rear office where the person believed to have committed the offence had been held. On arrival the female was being supervised by one single security guard employed by the venue. The question do you admit to the offence was put to the female, to which she denied all knowledge. The venue manager then informed the officers that there was supporting CCTV of the incident. The officer reviewed the footage which clearly showed the detained female kick the handbag away from the victim, pick the item up then pass it off to another female who then left with a larger group of females. The officer noted the descriptions and direction of travel of the females, temporarily exiting the venue to relay this information in a timely fashion to the control room and other officers in order to request observations for them. The group was located soon after and were then held by security within the complex area, they were fully compliant at this time. The officers dealing with the request relayed to the control room and to the operational supervisor that they had reviewed the CCTV and warranted the entire group being held and the police called. The officers request for this was declined, the reason given was that the supervising officer in the control room had not reviewed the CCTV. The alleged victim who was distraught by the ordeal was then advised by the responding officer on scene to contact the Police to report the incident. The girl who was initially detained at the venue was then released into the custody of the complex security personnel. The officers on scene again asked for the complex to secure this female and her friends as the CCTV had been reviewed and it clearly showed an indictable offence had been committed. Again this request was denied, and the officers told to take them to a seated customer service area and standby. The females all refused to give any personal details and were at this time voluntarily waiting quite compliantly. They were informed that there is CCTV of the incident and the police are en-route, to which they offered no response. The control room then received a call that a bag was seen hidden behind a planter in the complex. This information was relayed to the responding officer who made his way with the victim to that location. The bag was recovered and confirmed as the victims however it was minus her purse and mobile phone. This information was relayed to control and the officer then returned to the location where the alleged suspects were held. On his arrival all the suspects were gone. He was then informed by other officers that the supervising manager had rang on the land line and informed those at the scene to take their names and release them, which they did.

De-brief:

This incident should have run smoothly. There was an identified victim, a team of suspects and clear continuity of CCTV evidence to back it up. There was a secure holding area which was not used, which increases the risk of them making off. Due to this resource not being used the alleged offenders came face to face with the alleged victim which caused further distress for the aggrieved party. It was not required for the supervisor to review the CCTV from the venue and this was not normally the case anyway. The supervisor should have followed the guidance of the officers on scene who were investigating and in possession of more of the facts, in the same way that when CCTV control has more information the officers rely on them. This exercise was not one in joined up thinking and was contrary to standard operating procedure. The supervisor was taking it on themselves to make decisions they were not permitted to make. As expected the alleged perpetrators all gave false names and addresses and were released before the police could arrive. The CCTV was passed to the police and on review it was confirmed that it clearly showed the offence. The females were never traced however there was additional footage obtained two weeks later when the same group returned and on entering made their way into the staff area of a retail unit and helped themselves to two iPhones before safely making off.

Hypothetical Training Situations

We are now going to look at some hypothetical scenario situations and review and examine possible options and outcomes for each. It is often not possible to find or have personal knowledge of every form of incident that we would like to review. Case Studies are an excellent means of assessing operational practice through the experience of others or after an event. But it is not practical to write a case study for all events as it is impossible to have experienced every type of incident which may present.

Whether you are still green around the gills or a seasoned professional you will at some point deal with something that is new to you. It is therefore wise to think about all possibilities and consider as many hypothetical situation as your imagination can come up with. This exercise will increase your thought processes and optimise your effectiveness at assessing threat and risk. Anything which promotes this will assist not only in the planning phase but also throughout a presented incident.

Scenario One

Drunken Individual

You are working in a hotel lobby, providing security and customer service when you see a well dressed man enter. He is staggering and looking confused. He makes no attempt to approach the desk and makes his way directly to the lifts.

Would you consider:

1) Averting your eyes and pretending you have not seen him.
2) Approach him, and whilst implementing SAFER, ask if he needs any assistance.
3) Monitor his actions and movements.

Review:

If you have answered (1) then you are not only wrong you also lack standards. You should be doing actions (2) & (3). Without making enquiries you won't know if the gentlemen's actions are due to intoxication or the result of a medical condition. Guessing when you have the ability to find out is foolish. He was staggering and appeared confused therefore you have a duty of care not only to him by the fact he is on the premises but also to other guests. If he is a guest he would have a room number. If he has a medical or alcohol related condition he will need assistance. Remember the licensing act in regard to these premises. Attempt to get as much detail as possible but above all be helpful and professional.

Scenario Two

Building Structural Damage

The venue in which you are working has sustained structural damage due to an overnight storm. The damage is not excessive and does not impact the operational ability of the premises however it is in a public area and poses a threat to safety.

Consider actions:

1) Confirm the hazard has been reported and is being actioned.
2) Make use of cones, tape, barriers, signs and cordon area.
3) Can the area be fully closed & foot traffic redirected.
4) Remove the risk of further injury & make safe.
5) Any other considerations

Scenario Three

Missing Person

You are employed as a patrol officer at a leisure venue. On duty you are approached by an elderly female who informs you that she has become separated from her husband and has been looking for him for an hour to no avail. She is understandably extremely agitated.

Consider actions:

1) Empathise and try and calm and reassure.
2) Obtain an A to H description of the misper (missing person).
3) Does he have any medical conditions that may have a bearing (emotional/physical/mental) (concern for welfare)
4) Exact time and location last seen.
5) Possible direction of travel and background as to places he intended to visit on site.
6) How did you arrive? It may be possible that he has returned to vehicle/bus stop or even home if close by.
7) Does he have a mobile phone and have you tried ringing it. Is there anyone at home that he may have contacted.
8) Arrange for CCTV/physical sweeps to be carried out.
9) If required, as a concern for welfare, report it to the police.

Scenario Four

Intoxicated Patron

You are employed by a Public House in the capacity of Door Supervisor. A patron is obviously heavily in drink and their behaviour becomes increasingly unacceptable. You observe this and inform a colleague you intend to ask this person to leave. You approach the person in question and advise them that due to their conduct you require them to leave the premises. The person fully complies, staggering towards the door and stepping through and out onto the street. However this former patron does not walk far but remains standing approximately 15 – 20 metres away from the premises, and whilst inside when you spoke to them they became quite sheepish and willing to comply, this is no longer the case in the fresh air. The person is now rather annoyed regarding his ejection and is now shouting, swearing and goading you and your colleagues in the road and generally causing a public nuisance.

Would you consider:

1) Offering to call him a taxi.
2) Entering into a verbal altercation with him.
3) Walking towards him in order to move him on.
4) Displaying anger in order not to appear to lose face.
5) Avoiding verbal interaction whilst continuing to monitor for aggression indicators and reassessment variables.
6) Consider contacting police to alert them as a concern for welfare.
7) Advise other venues and CCTV in the area via pub watch radio, passing details of location and direction of travel, actions & description.

Review:

Avoiding points (2) (3) and (4) should be obvious. By entering into any kind of communication with this person above and beyond that which is required only gives him ammunition to validate his position. Point (3) would be totally unnecessary unless he posed an imminent threat to himself or someone else. If you walk towards him on the public highway and he is not in your red zone nor poses any danger then you could be considered the aggressor and would affect any justification issues should physical intervention be required as a result. By offering to call the gentlemen a taxi at the outset is a nice customer service gesture and often goes a long way to calming any escalation.

Should the situation deteriorate you can more easily justify any lawful action by demonstrating you did all you could to help minimise risk. By monitoring and reassessing along with advising other bars, CCTV and if needed the police, you are not only assisting public protection but at the same time prioritising a concern for welfare towards the individual.

Scenario Five

Medical Emergency

You are on patrol at a music concert when you witness a crowd forming in an area. You alert your colleagues and make your way to investigate. As you get there you see a young woman collapsed. She is breathing and conscious at this time but it is obvious she needs medical assistance. Unfortunately you have no first hand medical training.

You should:

1) Pass location and nature of the event to your control.
2) Request medical assistance if available or 999.
3) Remain and reassure the casualty till help arrives.
4) Inform those responding if the situation deteriorates or changes.
5) Advise others to clear the area in order to allow access for responders.
6) When help does arrive remain in that location. Help, assist and follow all instructions passed to you by the medical responder.
7) If the casualty has friends or family with them, reassure them and seek the personal details of the casualty on behalf of the medical responder, as all details must be recorded in accordance with all policies in relation to accident or injury.

Review:

All who work in the industry should have some formal medical training. However not all do and as a result a small number will attempt to either avoid helping or will relieve themselves of any responsibility by disappearing as soon as possible after help arrives. You may have little or no training or you may lack the confidence to deal with issues of a medical nature. This is not a problem and it is beneficial to inform others of this position in order that cover can be maintained. But it must be remembered that even those without medical experience and responsibilities still have to play a part. Every incident has to have a command and control structure, those with the skills and knowledge lead, and those without follow. In an emergency it should always be an all hands on deck approach and those lacking medical training should still offer support. By doing so it eases pressure on the first responders, while at the same time allows those providing support to observe, assist and learn.

CONCLUSION

From carrying out a review of the case studies you should now be aware of where things went well and where things did not. I use the word well as I consciously try to avoid using the word perfect or any derivative of it. Perfection is often out of reach and striving for perfection during an incident will often after the fact make you overly critical of your actions and those of others. Therefore I find using words like well, reactive and effective much better words to use, referring to events in regard to what went well and what did not allows your mind to remain receptive to change with any review and assessment focusing on improvement rather than blame.

Taking into account the scenarios, the challenges and options presented will get you thinking about the specific risks within the environment you operate in. By taking the time to actively think, writing your own scenarios and following the SAFER approach you will more easily visualise incidents and dilemmas occurring in familiar surroundings.

By adding a familiar setting to your training you will more easily absorb and understand your aims and objectives allowing you to recall what you are learning more easily. If you can expand this into a team activity; discussing, considering and even role-playing events all the better.

Throughout this book we have emphasised the importance of the individual operator's responsibility both in understanding the duties required and the need for continued self improvement. It is not possible nor wise to pin the responsibility for training and role definition on an employer or regulator. Task duties may well be controlled by an employer but implementation has to be formulated by the security professional entrusted to carry them out. Having the confidence to take ownership of what you do and to continually improve and expand your skill is the mark of an individual committed to minimizing risk. The industry must continually adapt in order to meet the challenges it faces, complacency is self defeating. Combine that with a limited commitment and a lacklustre approach and you are left with stagnant failure. This can and must be addressed and rectified by those on the front line. Only by changing attitudes and promoting professionalism on the ground can the industry be elevated.

When we consider regulation of the sector, the regulator must promote a principle of implementing core skills. But it is down to those of us who are in clear view of the public to promote the raising of standards. The individual professional must understand and accept the need for dynamic training, learning practices and evolve those practices into a conditioned response. It should be the front line professional that leads the way in regulation by demonstrating a higher standard and promoting values, lifting the industry and guiding its future. The current regulator has created an entry level base standard on which the industry must itself build. Finding fault with regulation is one thing, but doing so without accepting our own personal responsibility towards facilitating the problems perpetuates the issue. Robust training is required but that must be complemented by a robust and professional workforce.

We have in this book taken a look at the theory and core training principles of implementing a safety orientated role. One which comes into direct contact with hostility. By understanding the need to approach situations in a particular manner we can avoid or diffuse many of the risks we face. Through reading and absorbing the information held within this book you will be better placed to understand situations, assess them and respond. When it comes to guidelines and principles something which is often overlooked is the fact they they are put in place to steer, not lead you. Any guiding practice must be scrutinized and robustly tested in order to improve approach. However they can never supersede governing law.

Security may be considered a job. In reality it is known as a vocation by those with the commitment and foresight. Those which understand the risks and do all they can to reduce them. It is a unique quality in a person being able to put the safety of others equal to or above their own. This is something to be very proud of. Stepping towards danger while others step away is not a natural act. It requires strength of character and dedication to duty, battling through the fear to do what's right. Security is a valuable service, a service dedicated to protecting people and property. The preservation of life is the ultimate duty. A security provider requires the ability to make split second judgements, whilst projecting professional integrity and an ethical belief which goes far beyond what many expect. It is a trade, one that requires commitment to master. You must learn through knowledge, wisdom and experience the realities of the industry. An industry, a professional body like any team is only as strong as its weakest link. Taking ownership of the problem and addressing it is not something confined to others it is the duty of all. Assessment is not just an operational concern it is an industry one to. Meeting the challenges that we face must be done head on, and done at all levels. Committing as an individual to the raising of standards will promote continued growth not only in the abilities of the individual operator but by demonstrating this to others will also raise the standards of the industry and its perception within society. This growth will not only protect others from threat but will also protect you from repercussions.

www.ingramcontent.com/pod-product-compliance
Lightning Source LLC
Chambersburg PA
CBHW071344280526
45787CB00001B/210